GREAT ARTISTS COLLECTION

FIVE CENTURIES OF GREAT ART

by William Gaunt

ENCYCLOPAEDIA BRITANNICA : LONDON

Volume twenty

© 1971 by Phaidon Press Limited, London

This revised edition published in 1972
by Encyclopaedia Britannica International Limited, London

ISBN 0 85229 120 5

Printed in Great Britain

Contents

Introduction

Great Painters in their Historical Setting

The aim of this Linking Volume to the Great Artists Collection is to provide a concise account of the broad history of European painting, from the Renaissance to the early twentieth century.

After centuries of neglect, Botticelli (see page 13, and Volume 4) was rediscovered in the second half of the nineteenth century. He has since become one of the most popular of fifteenth-century Florentine painters. The delicacy of his imagination and the suppleness of his draughtsmanship are nowhere better displayed than in the *Birth of Venus* (Volume 4, Plates 29 and 30); Venus herself, indeed, has become as famous as her Hellenistic counterpart, the *Venus de Milo*.

From Botticelli, we move on to those twin giants of the High Renaissance: Leonardo da Vinci (see page 19, and Volume 16) and Michelangelo (see pages 14 and 19, and Volume 17), both of whom belong to that very select group of creative geniuses (Mozart, Shakespeare, Homer, Dante and Titian also come to mind) whose works have remained fundamentally immune to the ebb and flow of taste. Leonardo is arguably the most prodigally gifted man that Europe has ever produced combining to an exceptional degree as he did, the analytic gifts of the scientist with the imaginative capacities and executive skill of the artist. That is why you will find reproduced a series of his drawings (Volume 16, Plates 32–48), which reveal his strange and turbulent mind at work, ceaselessly experimenting, designing, inventing, seized by doubts and second thoughts. Leonardo is the first artist whom we can observe 'thinking aloud'. Michelangelo was not as versatile as Leonardo, but he was also unique in being the only artist of the first rank who has ever succeeded in being as great a sculptor as he was a painter. It is for this reason that we have devoted a section of plates (Volume 17, Plates 1–15 and 34–48) to some of his finest carvings, whose subtle textures are better recaptured in black and white than in colour.

At a first glance, there is a world of difference between Michelangelo's vast frescoes in the Sistine Chapel and the relatively small, crowded pictures of Pieter Bruegel (see page 26, and Volume 14). But at a deeper level, they are united in their deeply pessimistic view of the human race. It is very interesting to compare the *Last Judgement* (Figure 4, and Volume 17, Plate 26) with Bruegel's *Triumph of Death* (Figure 16, and Volume 14, Plates 6 and 11).

Since the end of the thirteenth century, European artists had been preoccupied with the problems of how to represent the world about them accurately. In the seventeenth century, painters began to depict, more seriously and more consistently than ever before, the play of light on figures, objects and even landscapes. A fascination with the effects of light on surfaces and textures is one of the strongest links between three of the age's greatest artists: Rubens (see pages 29 and 30, and Volume 10), Velazquez (see pages 50–1 and 53, and Volume 12) and Rembrandt (see pages 35–8, and Volume 3). Another bond is their common interest in portraiture.

Although Great Britain had produced Chaucer and the supreme figure of Shakespeare, it was not really until the eighteenth century that a national school of painting worthy of the name emerged. And since—both before and after that period—it was often in portraiture that the British artist excelled (see pages 58–62), it was decided to include an exciting anthology of portraits, either by British artists or, in some cases, by resident foreign painters such as Holbein and Van Dyck (see Volume 13).

The two most famous British portrait-painters of the eighteenth century, Gainsborough (died 1788) and Reynolds (died 1792), painted sitters from many different walks of life. Far away, in Spain, there lived a painter of society portraits who had even studied prints of Gainsborough's pictures. But had either Reynolds or Gainsborough seen the portraits painted in the 1780s by Goya (1746–1828), they would hardly have predicted his future development. For Goya (Volume 6)—like Beethoven, tragically afflicted by deafness—was caught up in a maelstrom of war and revolution, and emerged as one of the most savage commentators on the human scene in the history of European art. Can you imagine a less flattering royal portrait than the famous *Charles IV and his Family* (Volume 6, Plate 15)? In the uninhibited freedom with which he explored the recesses of his bitter imagination, and in the way he defended his integrity as an artist, Goya can be seen as a quintessential figure of Romanticism, that great movement— part philosophy, part life-style, part artistic expression—which dominated the mind and imagination of western man in the first half of the nineteenth century.

One of the chief tenets of Romanticism was a cult of nature as a source of wisdom as much as of aesthetic inspiration (the famous song, *Trees*, exemplifies an attitude that gained currency with the Romantic Movement). And it is this mood, this sense of the natural world discovered with rapture, as if for the first time, that unites Turner (see pages 68–70, and Volume 19) and Constable (see pages 68–71, and Volume 2). In one of Constable's most celebrated paintings a stretch of unpretentious Suffolk countryside and a humble cart are accorded a respect they had rarely enjoyed before; and that is why *The Haywain* (Volume 2, Plates 24 and 43), as well as being very beautiful, is also a very serious picture indeed.

This respect for the ordinary world, and the passion with which they tried to capture and pin down on canvas the fleeting effects of sunlight and cloud, storm and rain, are what attracted the French Impressionists to Constable and Turner. They, too, were deeply committed to the problem of how to paint the scenery and scenes of daily life. Unlike their English predecessors, however, Renoir (see pages 81–2, and Volume 9), Manet (see pages 75–7, and Volume 8) and Van Gogh (see pages 85 and 89, and Volume 1) were also strongly interested in painting human beings and still-life. In their search for an art that would be more 'truthful', they also experimented with new methods of design, and were much influenced by the boldness and simplicity, the freedom from the restraints of the European academic tradition, evident in the Japanese prints that were beginning to be imported from the Far East. Quite apart from their own exquisite qualities, this connection with Impressionism makes Japanese colour prints (see page 78, and Volume 7) especially interesting to us today.

Some of the visual boldness and a comparable feeling for pattern is to be found in the work of Paul Gauguin (see pages 85–6, and Volume 15), who, together with Seurat (see pages 85–8, and Volume 11) and Cézanne (see pages 85–6, and Volume 5), belongs to a later phase of Impressionism, usually known as Post-Impressionism.

Looking through your nineteen volumes, and as you casually turn over the pages, pausing every now and then to study a favourite painting, you may come to feel that the artists of earlier ages made up for deficiencies in technique by achieving a degree of serenity that becomes less common as we approach our own times. There is something in this: there can be no doubt that art, like the world it mirrors, has become more restless and more prone to doubts and violent convulsions than was the case five hundred years ago. But restlessness has its positive side when it is an aspect of vitality. And who has shown more vitality, greater inventiveness, more originality, in the seventy years in which he has been constantly at work, than Picasso? Pablo Picasso (see pages 90–1, and Volume 18) proves—if proof is needed—that art can still be as exciting, as vivid, as thought-provoking and inspiring, as it was in the days when Botticelli transformed simple Florentine children into angels, to stand beside the Virgin Mary and her Child.

1. The Spirit of the Renaissance in Italy

Like other movements of importance in art, the Renaissance, or *Rinascimento*, was so titled when it was nearing its end in the sixteenth century or at all events undergoing change of a drastic kind. The idea of 'rebirth' or 'revival' was patriotically satisfying to Italians. It implied that the traditions of the classical world of which Rome was the imperial centre were restored. The intrusion of the 'Middle Ages' (a term which came into use about the same time), a barrier interposed by the northern 'barbarism' of Gothic on the one hand and the oriental formalism of the Byzantine Empire on the other, had been removed. Yet the spirit of the Renaissance already existed in medieval times. It was fostered by the post-feudal growth of the independent city.

A typical constitution is to be found both in the cities of Italy and the cities of the southern Netherlands. Grown wealthy through commerce and industry, they had a democratic organization of guilds, though democracy was kept in check as a rule by some rich and powerful individual or family. A close comparison may be drawn between Florence and Bruges in the fifteenth century. They were twin pillars of European trade and finance. Art and decorative craft flourished: in the Flemish city with the patronage of the Dukes of Burgundy and the wealthy merchants as well as of the Church; in Florence with that of the millionaire Medici family.

In this congenial atmosphere, painters took an increasing interest in the representation of the visible world instead of being confined to that exclusive concern with the spirituality of religion that could only be given visual form in symbols and rigid conventions. The change, sanctioned by the tastes and liberal attitude of patrons (including sophisticated churchmen) is already apparent in Gothic painting of the later Middle Ages, and culminates in what is known as the International Gothic style of the fourteenth century and the beginning of the fifteenth. Throughout Europe—in France, Flanders, Germany, Italy and Spain—painters, freed from monastic disciplines, displayed the main characteristics of this style in the stronger narrative interest of their religious paintings, the effort to give more humanity of sentiment and appearance to the Madonna and other revered images, more individual character to portraiture in general and to introduce details of landscape, animal and bird life that the painter-monk of an earlier day would have thought all too mundane. These, it may be said, were characteristics also of Renaissance painting, but a vital difference appeared early in the fifteenth century. Such representatives of the International Gothic as Simone di Martini (1283–1344) at Siena and the Umbrian-born Gentile da Fabriano (1360–1428) were still ruled by the idea of making an elegant surface design with a bright, unrealistic pattern of colour. The realistic aim of a succeeding generation involved the radical step of penetrating through the surface to give a new sense of space, recession and three-dimensional form.

This decisive advance in realism first appeared about the same time in Italy and the Netherlands, more specifically in the work

I. FLORENCE. Piazza della Signoria: Loggia dei Lanzi.

1. MASACCIO. Adam and Eve Driven out of Paradise. About 1427. Florence, S. Maria del Carmine.

of Masaccio (1401–1428) at Florence, and of Jan van Eyck (c. 1390–1441) at Bruges. Masaccio, who in his short life was said by Delacroix to have brought about by his own efforts the greatest revolution that painting had ever known, gave a new impulse to Florentine art in his frescoes in the Brancacci Chapel of Santa Maria del Carmine (Fig. 1). The figures in these narrative compositions seemed to stand and move in ambient space; they were modelled with something of a sculptor's feeling for three dimensions, while gesture and expression were varied in a way that established not only the different characters of the persons depicted, but also their interrelation. In this respect he anticipated the special study of Leonardo in the *Last Supper* and in grandeur of manner had inspiration to give to the Raphael of *The School of Athens* in the Vatican.

Though Van Eyck also created a new sense of space and vista, there is an obvious difference between his work and that of Masaccio which also illuminates the distinction between the remarkable Flemish school of the fifteenth century and the Italian *quattrocento*. Both could be admired then as equally 'modern' but they were distinct in medium and idea. Italy had a long tradition of mural painting in fresco, which in itself made for a certain largeness of style, whereas the Netherlandish painter, working in an oil medium on panels of relatively small size, retained some of the minuteness of the miniature painter. Masaccio, indeed, was not a lone innovator but one who carried farther the fresco narrative tradition of his great forerunner at Florence, Giotto (1266?–1337).

Florence had a different orientation also as a centre of classical learning and philosophic study. The city's intellectual vigour made it the principal seat of the Renaissance in the fifteenth century and was an influence felt in every art. Scholars who devoted themselves to the study and translation of classical texts, both Latin and Greek, were the tutors in wealthy and noble households that came to share their literary enthusiasm. This in turn created the desire for pictorial versions of ancient history and legend. The painter's range of subject was greatly extended in consequence and he now had further problems of representation to solve in addition to those set by the effort to infuse humanity and reality into the subject of Christian import.

In this way, what might have been simply a nostalgia for the past and a retrograde step in art became a move forward and an exciting process of discovery. The human body, so long excluded from painting and sculpture by religious scruple—except in the most meagre and unrealistic form—gained a new importance in the portrayal of the gods, goddesses and heroes of classical myth. Painters had to become reacquainted with anatomy, to understand the relation of bone and muscle, the dynamics of movement. In the picture now treated as a stage instead of a flat plane, it was necessary to explore and make use of the science of perspective. In addition, the example of classical sculpture was an incentive to combine naturalism with an ideal of perfect proportion and physical beauty.

Painters and sculptors in their own fashion asserted the dignity of man as the humanist philosophers did, and evinced the same thirst for knowledge. Extraordinary indeed is the list of great Florentine artists of the fifteenth century and, not least extraordinary, the number of them that practised more than one art or form of expression.

In every way the remarkable Medici family fostered the intellectual climate and the developments in the arts that made Florence the mainspring of the Renaissance. The fortune derived from the banking house founded by Giovanni de' Medici (*c.* 1360–

1429), with sixteen branches in the cities of Europe, was expended on this promotion of culture, especially by the two most distinguished members of the family, Cosimo, Giovanni's son (1389–1464), and his grandson Lorenzo (1448–92), who in their own gifts as men of finance, politics and diplomacy, their love of books, their generous patronage of the living and their appreciation of antiques of many kinds, were typical of the universality that was so much in the spirit of the Renaissance.

The equation of the philosophy of Plato and Christian doctrine in the academy instituted by Cosimo de' Medici seems to have sanctioned the division of a painter's activity, as so often happened, between the religious and the pagan subject. The intellectual atmosphere the Medici created was an invigorating element that caused Florence to outdistance neighbouring Siena. Though no other Italian city of the fifteenth century could claim such a constellation of genius in art, those that came nearest to Florence were the cities likewise administered by enlightened patrons. Lodovico Gonzaga (1414–78), Marquess of Mantua, was a typical Renaissance ruler in his aptitude for politics and diplomacy, in his encouragement of humanist learning and in the cultivated taste that led him to form a great art collection and to employ Andrea Mantegna (1431–1506) as court painter.

Of similar calibre was Federigo Montefeltro, Duke of Urbino. Like Lodovico Gonzaga, he had been a pupil of the celebrated humanist teacher, Vittorino da Feltre, whose school at Mantua combined manly exercises with the study of Greek and Latin authors and inculcated the humanist belief in the all-round improvement possible to man. At the court of Urbino, which set the standard of good manners and accomplishment described by Baldassare Castiglione in *Il Cortigiano*, the Duke entertained a number of painters, principal among them the great Piero della Francesca (1410/20–92).

The story of Renaissance painting after Masaccio brings us first to Fra Angelico (1387–1455), born earlier but living much longer. Something of the Gothic style remains in his work but the conventual innocence, which is perhaps what first strikes the eye, is accompanied by a mature firmness of line and sense of structure. This is evident in such paintings of his later years as *The Adoration of the Magi* now in the Louvre and the frescoes illustrating the lives of St. Stephen and St. Lawrence, frescoed in the Vatican for Pope Nicholas V in the late 1440s. They show him to have been aware of, and able to turn to advantage, the changing and broadening attitude of his time. His pupil Benozzo Gozzoli (*c.* 1421–97) nevertheless kept to the gaily decorative colour and detailed incident of the International Gothic style in such a work as the panoramic *Procession of the Magi* in the Palazzo Riccardi, Florence, in which he introduced the equestrian portrait of Lorenzo de' Medici.

Nearer to Fra Angelico than Masaccio was Fra Filippo Lippi (1406–69), a Carmelite monk in early life and a protégé of Cosimo de' Medici, who looked indulgently on the artist's various

2. FRA FILIPPO LIPPI. Madonna and Child. About 1460. Florence, Uffizi.

3. BOTTICELLI. Head of Venus. Detail from 'The Birth of Venus'. About 1486. Florence, Uffizi.

escapades, amorous and otherwise. Fra Filippo, in the religious subjects he painted exclusively, both in fresco and panel, shows the tendency to celebrate the charm of an idealized human type that contrasts with the urge of the fifteenth century towards technical innovation. He is less distinctive in purely aesthetic or intellectual quality than in his portrayal of the Madonna as an essentially feminine being (Fig. 2). His idealized model, who was slender of contour, dark-eyed and with raised eyebrows, slightly retroussé nose and small mouth, provided an iconographical pattern for others. A certain wistfulness of expression was perhaps transmitted to his pupil, Sandro Botticelli (1446–1510).

In Botticelli's paintings much of the foregoing development of the Renaissance is summed up. He excelled in that grace of feature and form that Fra Filippo had aimed to give and of which Botticelli's contemporary, Ghirlandaio (1449–94), also had his delightful version in frescoes and portraits. He interpreted in a unique pictorial fashion the neo-Platonism of Lorenzo de' Medici's humanist philosophers. The network of ingenious allegory in which Marsilio Ficino, the tutor of Lorenzo di Pierfrancesco de' Medici (a cousin of Lorenzo the Magnificent), sought to demonstrate a relation between Grace, Beauty and Faith, has equivalent subtlety in *Primavera* and *The Birth of Venus* (Fig. 3) executed for Lorenzo's villa. The poetic approach to the classics of Angelo Poliziano, also a tutor of the Medici family, may be seen reflected in Botticelli's art. Though his span of life extended into the period of the High Renaissance, he still represents the youth of the movement in his delight in clear colours and exquisite natural detail. Perhaps in the wistful beauty of his Aphrodite something may be found of the nostalgia for the Middle Ages towards which, eventually, when Savonarola denounced the Medici and all their works, he made his passionate gesture of return.

The nostalgia as well as the purity of Botticelli's linear design, as yet unaffected by emphasis on light and shade, made him the especial object of Pre-Raphaelite admiration in the nineteenth century. But, as in other Renaissance artists, there was an energy in him that imparted to his linear rhythms a capacity for intense emotional expression as well as a gentle refinement. The distance of the Renaissance from the inexpressive calm of the classical period as represented by statues of Venus or Apollo, resides in this difference of spirit or intention even if unconsciously revealed. The expression of physical energy which at Florence took the form, naturally enough, of representations of the male nude, gives an unclassical violence to the work of Antonio Pollaiuolo (1426–98).

Pollaiuolo was one of the first artists to dissect human bodies in order to follow exactly the play of bone, muscle and tendon in the living organism, with such dynamic effects as appear in the muscular tensions of struggle in his bronze of *Hercules and Antaeus* (Florence, Bargello) and the movements of the archers in his painting *The Martyrdom of St. Sebastian* (London, National Gallery). Luca Signorelli (*c.* 1441–1523), though associated with

4. MICHELANGELO. The Damned. Detail from 'The Last Judgement'. 1536–41. Rome, Vatican, Sistine Chapel.

the Umbrian School as the pupil of Piero della Francesca, was strongly influenced by the Florentine Pollaiuolo in his treatment of the figure. With less anatomical subtlety but with greater emphasis on outward bulges and striations of muscle and sinew, he too aimed at dynamic effects of movement, obtaining them by sudden explosions of gesture.

It was a direction of effort that seems to lead naturally and inevitably to the achievement of Michelangelo (1475–1564). Though there are manifest differences in mode of thought and style between his *Last Judgement* in the Sistine Chapel (Fig. 4) and Signorelli's version in the frescoes in Orvieto Cathedral (Fig. 5), they have in common a formidable energy. It was a quality which made them appear remote from the balance and harmony of classical art. Raphael (1483–1520) was much nearer to the classical spirit in the Apollo of his *Parnassus* (Fig. 6) in the Vatican and the *Galatea* in the Farnesina, Rome. One of the most striking of the regional contrasts of the Renaissance period is between the basically austere and intellectual character of art in Tuscany in the rendering of the figure as compared with the sensuous languor

5. SIGNORELLI. The Last Judgement.
1499–1502. Orvieto Cathedral.

6. RAPHAEL. Apollo and the Muses. Detail
from 'The Parnassus'. 1508–11. Rome,
Vatican, Stanza della Segnatura.

7. GIORGIONE. 'The Tempest'. 1506–8. Venice, Accademia.

8. TITIAN. Venus of Urbino. 1538. Florence, Uffizi.

of the female nude as painted in Venice by Giorgione (Fig. 7) (1477/8–1520) and Titian (Fig. 8) (1480/90–1576). Though even in this respect Florentine science was not without its influence. The soft gradation of shadow devised by Leonardo da Vinci to give subtleties of modelling (Fig. 9) was adopted by Giorgione and at Parma by Correggio (c. 1489–1534) as a means of heightening the voluptuous charm of a Venus, an Antiope (Fig. 10) or an Io.

The Renaissance masters not only made a special study of anatomy but also of perspective, mathematical proportion and, in general, the science of space. The omnivorous desire of the period for knowledge may partly account for this abstract pursuit, but it had more specific origins and reasons. Perspective was firstly the study of architects in drawings and reconstructions of the classical types of building they sought to revive. In this respect, the great architect Filippo Brunelleschi (1377–1446) was a leader in his researches in Rome. In Florence he gave a demonstration of perspective in a drawing of the piazza of San Giovanni that awakened the interest of other artists, his friend Masaccio in particular. The architect Alberti (1404–72) was another propagator of the scientific theory. Painters concerned with a picture as a three-dimensional illusion realized the importance of perspective as a contribution to the effect of space.

Paolo Uccello (1397–1475) was one of the early promoters of the

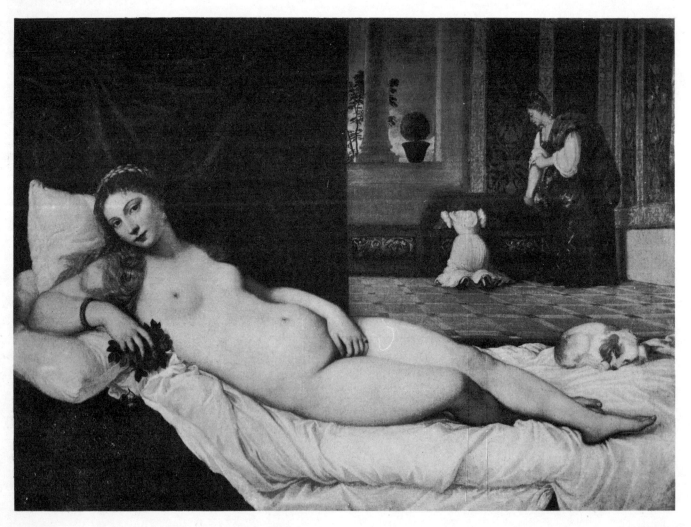

9. LEONARDO DA VINCI. Detail. Madonna and Child with St. Anne. Cartoon. About 1507. London, National Gallery.

science at Florence. His painting of *The Battle of San Romano* in the National Gallery, London, with its picturesqueness of heraldry, is a beautifully calculated series of geometric forms and mathematical intervals. Even the broken lances on the ground seem so arranged as to lead the eye to a vanishing point. His foreshortening of a knight prone on the ground was an exercise of skill that Andrea Mantegna was to emulate. It was Mantegna who brought the new science of art to Venice.

In the complex interchange of abstract and mathematical ideas and influences, Piero della Francesca stands out as the greatest personality. Though an Umbrian, born at the little town of Borgo San Sepolcro, he imbibed the atmosphere of Florence and Florentine art as a young man, when he worked there with the Venetian-born Domenico Veneziano (*c.* 1400–61). Domenico had

10. CORREGGIO. The Sleep of Antiope. 1521–2. Paris, Louvre.

assimilated the Tuscan style and had his own example of perspective to give, as in the beautiful *Annunciation* now in the Fitzwilliam Museum, Cambridge, though Piero probably gained his scientific attitude towards design from the three pioneers of research, Brunelleschi, Alberti and Donatello.

The contrast of elements in Piero's art is part of its fascination. The grace of Fra Angelico, the Florentine delight in personal beauty, left their trace in his painting. The angelic choir of *The Nativity* (Fig. 11) in the National Gallery brings to mind the youthful singers of the Cantoria in the Cathedral at Florence by Luca della Robbia (1399–1482). At the same time there was the abstract intellect at work, mathematically calculating planes, geometrically simplifying forms, with a resulting grandeur that appears in Piero's frescoes at Arezzo and in so awe-inspiring a masterpiece as the *Resurrection* at Borgo San Sepolcro.

Classical in ordered design and largeness of conception, but without the touch of antiquarianism that is to be found in

11. PIERO DELLA FRANCESCA. Detail of Angels from 'The Nativity'. 1474–8. London, National Gallery.

Mantegna, Piero was an influence on many painters. His interior perspectives of Renaissance architecture which added an element of geometrical abstraction to his figure compositions were well taken note of by his Florentine contemporary, Andrea del Castagno (*c.* 1421–57). A rigidly geometrical setting is at variance with and yet emphasizes the flexibility of human expression in the Apostles in Andrea's masterpiece *The Last Supper* (Fig. 12) in the Convent of Sant' Apollonia, Florence. Antonello da Messina (*c.* 1430–79) who introduced the Flemish technique of oil painting to the Venetian painters brought also a sense of form derived from Piero della Francesca that in turn was stimulating in its influence on Giovanni Bellini (*c.* 1430–1516), diverting him from a hard linear style like that of Mantegna and contributing to his mature greatness as leader of the Venetian school.

Of the whole wonderful development of the Italian Renaissance in the fifteenth century, Leonardo da Vinci and Michelangelo were the heirs. The universality of the artist was one remarkable aspect of the century. Between architect, sculptor, painter, craftsman and man of letters there had been no rigid distinction. Alberti was architect, sculptor, painter, musician, and writer of treatises on the theory of the arts. Verrocchio (1435–88), master of Leonardo, is described as a goldsmith, painter, sculptor and musician: and in sculpture could vie with any master. In a supreme degree Leonardo and Michelangelo displayed this universality. Leonardo, the engineer, the prophetic inventor, the learned student of nature in every aspect, the painter of haunting masterpieces, has never failed to excite wonder (Fig. 13). As much may

12. ANDREA DEL CASTAGNO. The Last Supper. 1445–50. Florence, Convent of S. Apollonia.

13. Leonardo da Vinci. The Last Supper. 1495–7. Milan, S. Maria delle Grazie.

be said of Michelangelo, the sculptor, painter, architect and poet. With the means perfected by their brilliant predecessors they expressed with even more of grandeur the power of mind. The crown of Florentine achievement, they also mark the decline of the city's greatness. Rome, restored to splendour by ambitious popes after long decay, claimed Michelangelo, together with Raphael, to produce the monumental conceptions of the High Renaissance. Leonardo, absorbed in his researches like Uccello and Piero della Francesca, was finally lured away to France. Yet in these great men the genius of Florence lived on.

2. *The Flemish Genius*

The dramatic changes of two centuries after the first great period of Flemish painting are signalized by the work of Pieter Bruegel the Elder (*c*. 1525–69) and Peter Paul Rubens (1577–1640). There was firstly an internal change in which economics and geography had their part. In the fifteenth century, artists had been attracted to Bruges and its prosperous neighbouring cities by the patronage they offered. The patrons included the wealthy merchants, who gained social prestige and credit for piety as donors of religious art to churches and convents; the members of the Burgundian court who delighted in colour and fine detail; and visitors from all over Europe who came to Bruges, the centre of international trade and finance, and bought pictures and illuminated manuscripts at the yearly fairs where these were among the most popular objects exhibited for sale.

The fame of the cities of Flanders and Brabant as centres of art was upheld by painters who were not necessarily Flemish by birth but came from different parts of the Netherlands. Jan van Eyck was born at Maaseyck in Limbourg and worked for some time at The Hague before entering the service of Duke Philip the Good of Burgundy and settling at Bruges. Though he later became closely associated with Bruges, Hans Memlinc (*c*. 1435–94) was a native of Seligenstadt, near Mainz. Dirck Bouts (*c*. 1410–75) came southwards from Haarlem to work at Brussels and Louvain, and Roger van der Weyden (*c*. 1399–1464) from Tournai.

There resulted the unique fusion in the first great period of northern and southern elements, of the realism characteristic of the Dutch and German painters and the decorative luxury derived from the Franco-Flemish art of the illuminated manuscript. But a series of misfortunes marks the decline of Bruges towards the end of the fifteenth century. The channel of the Zwijn —her access to the sea and sea-borne trade—silted up and became closed to navigation. The unsuccessful effort to get rid of the tyrannical Archduke Maximilian, who had married Marie of Burgundy, resulted in the city's being burdened with a huge indemnity and unable to undertake such extensive works as would restore her trading position. Meanwhile, shipping was diverted to Antwerp which became prosperous as never before, replacing Bruges as a port, a centre of financial operations and a city of culture.

Artists followed the movement of commerce. Humanist scholars at Antwerp introduced the thought and learning of the Renaissance, later disseminated in book form by the printing house of Christophe Plantin. How the altered circumstances might affect painters is clearly seen in the career of Quentin Metsys (1466–1530). Born at Louvain, son of the city architect who was also a metalworker and clockmaker, he made Antwerp the city of his choice and was one of the earliest artist settlers from elsewhere, becoming a master in the Antwerp painters' guild in 1491.

For the young artist it must have been like stepping into a new era. He now moved in intellectual circles, was the friend of Erasmus who commissioned him to paint the portrait of the

II. JAN VAN EYCK. Arnolfini Wedding Portrait. 1434. National Gallery, London.

English humanist, Sir Thomas More. Something remained in Metsys' paintings of religious subjects of the tradition on which Van Eyck had laid his indelible stamp, of Van der Weyden and Dirck Bouts; yet inevitably he fell in with the spirit of Antwerp, cognizant of a newly-discovered world, with enlarged horizons, respectful also of the mighty achievements of the Renaissance in Italy at its height. A departure from the dedicated gravity of the fifteenth-century masters is apparent in Metsys' work: there is a more intimate sense of the beauty and interest of the visible world and also a certain Italianate element. A likeness to the type of feminine countenance portrayed by Leonardo da Vinci has been frequently remarked on in his madonnas and saints, distinguished by the heavy-lidded eyes, the oval contours and the delicacy of shadow that gives a subtle gradation.

This may imply that he visited Italy, though of such a visit there seems no record. The borrowing, if such it was, does not give the effect of slavish imitation: and as a painter of *genre*, Metsys struck out in an entirely original line. His pictures of the banker or the usurer and wife (Fig. 14), counting coins and measuring precious metals in the scales, leave open the question whether they were simply the reflection of a moneyed society or a satire on its operations.

In either case, this combination of character study and still life was popular in sixteenth-century Antwerp. Metsys' two sons,

14. QUENTIN METSYS. The Banker and His Wife. 1514. Paris, Louvre.

Cornelius and Jan, also painters, practised the genre and, with more of a satirical aim, so did the Dutch painter settled at Antwerp, Marinus van Reymerswael. An indication is thus given of the growing favour now accorded the non-religious subject. Pieter Aertsen (1507–75), who came to Antwerp from Amsterdam, specialized in those market and kitchen scenes that later became a typical product of artists in Holland. His example was followed at Antwerp by his nephew by marriage, Joachim Beuckelaer (*c.* 1533–*c.* 1575).

Landscape was also coming into favour as a subject in its own right and not simply as the background of some devotional work. Joachim Patinir (*c.* 1480–1524), the pupil of Quentin Metsys, who came from Dinant seems to draw upon his memories of the Meuse in the panoramic river views in which Biblical episodes had only a token place. Their popularity is attested by the existing number of such works by him or by his imitators. An inducement also to paint landscape was the prospect that opened before the painter from the Netherlandish plain en route for Italy. It is a sign of the changed relations of the Netherlands and Italy that Flemish painters now went to Rome as pupils to learn from the great works of the later Renaissance, whereas in the century before they had had lessons to give. Then, Italian painters had profited by study of such a work as *The Adoration of the Shepherds* by Hugo van der Goes (*c.* 1440–82) which the agent of the Medici at Bruges, Tommaso Portinari, brought back to Florence. Joos van Wassenhove (Justus of Ghent), known in Italy as Giusto di Guanda, had worked on an equal footing at Urbino with Piero della Francesca. The background of distant landscape familiar in Flemish altarpieces was adopted by Piero with great effect in his double portrait of Federigo Montefeltro and his wife, now in the Uffizi. The style of donor portrait exemplified by the Portinari altarpiece was taken up in Florence.

Now that the earlier school had run its course, the Netherlands, like the rest of Europe outside Italy, sought to extract the secrets of classical grandeur contained in the works of Michelangelo and Raphael at Rome. Though Bruges still had its masters in the sixteenth century in Gerard David (*c.* 1460–1523), and his followers Ambrosius Benson and Adrien Isenbrandt, both active in the first half of the sixteenth century, they mark the close of a tradition by then confined in its late-medieval conventions. It was not Bruges or Ghent that interested Albrecht Dürer on his tour of the Netherlands in 1520 but Antwerp, a city of Renaissance character where he was greeted by kindred spirits among the painters and where he met the great humanist, Erasmus of Rotterdam. It was from Antwerp that the largest contingent of Netherlandish painters set out to cross the Alps and complete their education in the cities of Italy. The 'Romanists' as they came to be called did not find it altogether easy to assimilate the style and character of the High Renaissance. Jan Gossaert (*c.* 1475–1533), however, though tending to overelaborate, essayed a departure into classical mythology with some success. Bernard van

Orley (1488–1541) was one of those impressed by the Cartoons of
Raphael when they came to the weavers of Brussels (they are now
in the Victoria and Albert Museum, London), the influence of
Raphael being apparent in his altarpieces and own designs for
tapestry, though he was at his best in portraits most in accord with
the Flemish tradition.

Pieter Bruegel was among those who made the excursion to
Italy, but he seems to have remained impervious to the influence
of Italian art. He was more susceptible to the awesome heights and
rocky defiles of the Alpine landscape. They provided material for
the landscape prints he designed for the Antwerp engraver and
printseller, Jerome Cock, and memories to draw on for the superb
later paintings, his *Conversion of St. Paul*, for example. The main
links of his art otherwise were with the popular illustration of
proverbs and folk lore which Cock put out and with those who
showed an interest in national life, such as Pieter Aertsen. Yet the
term 'folk lore' must include the subjects engraved after the
fantasies of Jerome (or Hieronymus) Bosch whose strange genius
fascinated Bruegel to the point, realist though he was, of painting
in Bosch's manner. Of the extraordinary art of Bosch (*c.* 1450–
1516) there is no simple explanation. Nothing could be farther
than his universe of hallucination from the pictures of donors
kneeling in tranquil piety before the Virgin and Child that had
been the habitual product of the Flemish painter. What is known
of his life—which is little enough—gives no clue to the workings of
his mind. His time was uneventfully spent in the provincial town
of 's-Hertogenbosch. He was employed in the decoration of its
church, sang in the choir; was a member of the local benevolent
society, the Brotherhood of Our Lady; was married and had a
house in the market square, and a country property not far away.
Yet his paintings of sin and its punishment, of temptation and
torture by the most macabre of goblins in the weirdest of hells were
like no-one else's. How then was his imagination fed? Perhaps by
the dark superstitions left over from the past; by the Devil as
actors might represent him in the Brotherhood's mystery plays; by
studying works on alchemy and demonology; by membership of a
secret cult. A case can be made out for all these suppositions. On
the other hand he could be viewed more as a man of his own time,
interested in stories of a strange world of flora and fauna brought
back by travellers in that age of distant voyages and devising from
them his own pictures of weird and exotic life; and as one with an
attitude of satirical humanism to the follies and failings of mankind including those of the religious orders. Giving a pictorial
version of the poet Sebastian Brant's *Ship of Fools,* he did not spare
monks and nuns his satire.

What is beyond question is the genius that could invent the
amazing variety of hybrid demons that people his hell (Fig. 15),
and fill his 'garden of terrestrial delights' with its symbolic parade
of vice; not forgetting the mastery of the painter that could on
occasion add exquisite landscape; Bosch might also be thought
prophetic, in the lurid conflagrations of his triptychs, of the inferno

15. BOSCH. Detail from 'Hell', wing of triptych known as 'The Garden of Terrestrial Delights'. About 1500. Madrid, Prado.

16. PIETER BRUEGEL. Detail from 'The Triumph of Death'. About 1562. Madrid, Prado.

the Netherlands were for a time to become.

Luther nailed his theses against the papal indulgences to the door of Wittenberg cathedral the year after Bosch's death. It was not long before the defiant German priest had adherents in protest in all parts of the Netherlands; or before Charles V of whose overgrown empire the region was now a part took steps to put down the Protestant heresy.

The Burgundian connection had been the good fortune of the Netherlands—the Habsburg connection was their tragedy. Persecution began in earnest when in 1556 the Emperor abdicated and his son Philip II of Spain succeeded to the Habsburg dominions. Ruthless inquisitions, wholesale executions, the bitterly resented presence of Spanish troops are aspects of the grim background against which the art of Pieter Bruegel may be viewed. He painted the wonderful *Triumph of Death* (Fig. 16) (Madrid, Prado) just before the Duke of Alva entered Brussels in 1568 to extend the reign of terror.

The link with Bosch is clearly seen in Bruegel's more symbolic imaginings. His work represents also a new phase of the trend towards the secular subject and his greatness consisted in being at once universal and national. The Flemish technique was widened in scope to comprise the superb syntheses of Netherlandish plain and Alpine height that appears in the *Hunters in the Snow* (Vienna, Kunsthistorisches Museum) and that affectionately patriotic view of popular life (as opposed to the perilous court) that animates the realistic masterpieces of peasant life. It can hardly be doubted that the oppression of the time to which Bruegel makes covert references in such Biblical themes as *The Massacre of the Innocents* (also at Vienna) strengthened his national feeling. It turned into a warmth of new creation in which he surpasses Bosch, and by virtue of which he takes his place among the greatest European masters.

When Bruegel died, the limit of savagery and destruction had not yet been reached. The 'Spanish fury' of Alva's troops killing, looting, burning down buildings (including the Italianate Hôtel de Ville) had yet to burst on Antwerp. Bitter fighting was to go on for years. But by the beginning of the seventeenth century the independence of the northern provinces was an established fact. They had gathered together practically all the Lutheran and Calvinist elements of the population. Equally segregated were the Catholics and those acquiescent in Catholicism and foreign rule in the southern provinces.

Under the peaceable government of the Archduke Albert and his wife the Infanta Isabella, the south regained some of its old prosperity. Antwerp, though second now to the Dutch ports, kept a share of world trade. At Brussels, the capital, there was a court that maintained a front of gaiety but Antwerp was still the leading city of the arts. Painting was again a flourishing industry. The city was the home of an astonishing number of painters, born there for the most part and often constituting family dynasties. Most remarkable of any was the Bruegel family. After Pieter I came twenty-five descendants whose work spreads over three centuries, his two sons, Pieter II and Jan, being his immediate followers.

The demand that made for a great output in the first half of the seventeenth century came from several quarters. There was the demand for state portraiture which, as Anthonis Mor van Dashorst (1512–75) had shown somewhat earlier, could give the artist an entrée into many European courts. So international was this master of the Antwerp Guild that his name was variously translated as Antonio Moro and Sir Anthony More. As urgent as any was the requirement of the Catholic Church and its Jesuit action group—making the counter-attack against Protestantism—for altarpieces of a kind to strike the eye as forcibly as possible and at the same time to appeal strongly to the emotions.

Here the example of Italian art was followed and its influence can be traced from Mannerism in the art of the early Romanists, Frans Floris (de Vriendt) (1516–70), and Otto van Veen (1556–1629). The drama of Caravaggio's light and shade is reflected in the work of Abraham Janssens (1575–1632). Finally the Baroque in all its emotional force is given its Flemish form by Rubens (1577–1640), and Van Dyck (1599–1641) in his Antwerp period before he came to England. In landscape the vogue of the half realistic, half imaginary mountainous scenes popularized by such minor post-Bruegel painters as Tobias Verhaecht (1561–1631) and Joos de Momper (1564–1635) was continued by Paul Bril (1554–1626), Franz Wouters (1612–59), Lucas van Uden (1595–1672) and others. A number of other genres occupied painters. Flowers, always a delightful feature in Flemish pictures, gained a new importance (especially the tulip) in works answering to the contemporary interest in horticulture. A half-way between the flowerpiece and the devotional work were the floral garlands encircling some religious image in which the Jesuit, Daniel Seghers (1590–1661) specialized.

17. JORDAENS. Fecundity. About 1625.
Brussels, Musée des Beaux-Arts.

The courtiers at Brussels were entertained by interior views of their palaces and gardens, of their picture galleries with their collections and such themes as the Five Senses or the Four Elements in the symbolic form of flowers, fruit and still-life objects, which occupied a number of 'little masters'.

Towering above all at Antwerp was Rubens with the same lofty relation to his century as Bruegel in the century before. Excelling equally in altarpieces, for the churches of Antwerp and elsewhere; in allegories; in themes taken from classical mythology and ancient history; in landscapes; in portraits; in great decorative cycles such as the History of Maria de' Medici (Paris, Louvre); in hunting pieces and genre both courtly and peasant; he was stupendous in output and wonderfully efficient in organizing the division of labour among his many assistants.

He presided like some benevolent deity over helpers as able as Jacob Jordaens (1593–1678), who had much of his verve, though of a coarser quality (Fig. 17), Frans Snyders (1579–1657), akin to him in feeling for animal form, but with not so keen a sense of the dynamism of powerful beasts, and Jan Bruegel (1568–1625), the exquisite flower painter, with whom Rubens willingly collaborated on equal terms (Fig. 18). Add to this that he was a classical scholar, a linguist, a successful diplomat, a connoisseur and collector, of catholic taste, whose appreciation extended from antique marbles to the paintings of 'low life' by the successor to Bruegel, Adriaen Brouwer (1605–38); one who inspired a whole school of engravers

18. JAN BRUEGEL and RUBENS. Adam and Eve in Paradise. About 1620. The Hague, Mauritshuis.

19. RUBENS. Detail from 'War and Peace'. 1629–30. London, National Gallery.

as well as architects and sculptors; and the catalogue of his gifts and virtues becomes almost overwhelming.

In the course of his immensely productive career, his art developed naturally from the Romanist trend of his predecessors and the example of the Italian masters he studied so attentively during his stay in Italy. But Rubens remained essentially Flemish in the opulence of his form and in a lusty sense of life, light and colour (Fig. 19). What was lacking in the Baroque phase of art in the southern provinces that he and Van Dyck so superbly represent (Van Dyck, that is, in independent practice at Antwerp), is that contribution from the northern provinces which political and religious history had by then excluded. It has been said that the fifteenth century from Van Eyck to Memlinc was spiritual, the sixteenth century of Erasmus and Bruegel intellectual, and the century of Rubens sensual. It is a rough generalization that might call for amendment or qualification in various ways, but it serves as far as Rubens is concerned to distinguish the drama and gusto of his art from the puritanism of the north. Some critics have compared him to his disadvantage with artists more austere in religious expression, more refined in their ideal of physical beauty, more profound in implication of thought, but the torrent of his genius deprives such criticisms of much of their point. With him Flemish art came to its glorious close. The closing of the Scheldt to shipping required by the Treaty of Munster in 1648, only eight years after Rubens' death, put a terminus likewise of a material kind to Antwerp's golden age. But the influence of the master technician in colour and movement was to remain a vitalizing force in Europe, linking Rubens with great artists who came after him, from Watteau to Delacroix.

3. The Dutch Genius

III. GERRIT BERKEHYDE. View of Haarlem
with the Groote Kerk. 1674. Cambridge,
Fitzwilliam Museum.

As Rubens may be said to convey an essentially Flemish character in the sumptuous display and energy of his painting, so Rembrandt represents Holland in gravity of mood and concentrated intensity of expression. Difference of temperament between the northern and southern provinces of the Netherlands is clear in the contrast the two great artists provide, even though both tower above and in some respect are apart from their contemporaries. It was a difference less apparent in the art of an earlier period. In the fifteenth century the Netherlandish school we still refer to as Flemish comprised a number of Dutch painters but the free movement of artists from city to city, north and south, and the spread of the same stylistic influences, welded art into a non-regional unity.

A Dutch painter such as Geertgen tot Sint Jans, active in the second half of the fifteenth century at Haarlem, might, for all one could tell to the contrary, have been a follower of Van Eyck at Bruges. In the first half of the sixteenth century, Dutch and Flemish painters still tended to be more alike in their efforts to assimilate the lessons of the Italian Renaissance than regionally distinct, though Jan van Scorel (1495–1562) and Martin van Heemskerck (1498–1574) showed a special flair for realistic portraiture, of a type that foreshadows the art of seventeenth-century Holland.

The difference in character of the people generally was affirmed by the struggles between rulers and ruled, ending with what was effectively a victory for the Dutch in their fight for independence, the Twelve Year Truce of 1609. Determining factors were religion and patriotism, with an influence on art of the most decisive kind. The iconoclasm of the puritan resistance had destroyed much of Holland's legacy of religious art. Sculpture suffered to an extent that makes it hard now to realize that the Dutch had formerly excelled in its production. Many paintings of Christian themes in churches and convents had endured a like fate. A largely Protestant country, in principle, banned their replacement by others. The bare church interiors painted by Pieter Jansz Saenredam (1597–1665) and Emmanuel de Witte (1617–92) are reminders of the puritan attitude, contrasting with the profusion of religious images encouraged by the Jesuits in the Catholic south. The altarpieces that included the portrait of some wealthy burgess as donor were a thing of the past in Holland. The burgess now, singly, or in company with his family or as a member of a secular group, gained a new importance on canvas.

It must have been with a mixture of pride, relief, astonishment and delight that the Dutch surveyed their position in the opening years of the sixteenth century. Though Spain refused to admit defeat until the century was near the half-way mark, the Dutch had already won. They were free of a hated tyranny. The old provinces, united, formed a young nation, evoking an intense patriotic enthusiasm. The marvel was that far from being enfeebled by years of fighting, this newly-formed national entity was already powerful and rich by virtue of its ships and trade overseas.

The confident and carefree mood of the time is reflected in the phase of painting brilliantly represented by Frans Hals (*c.* 1580–1666) in his earlier years. The gaiety and joviality of the 1620s is mirrored in such paintings as *The Jolly Toper* (Amsterdam, Rijksmuseum) and the *Laughing Boy with Beer Jug* (Rotterdam, Boymans-van Beuningen Museum). He had a fondness for Bohemian types (Fig. 20). Hendrick Gerritz Pot (1585–1657), a fellow pupil of Hals under Carel van Mander (1548–1606) at Haarlem, painted 'merry companies' in Hals's style. Hals was adept in catching the consciousness of having lived in an heroic period which appears in the facial expression of the military or semi-military types he painted. An example is the so-called *Laughing Cavalier* of 1624 (London, Wallace Collection), whose self-satisfaction may be discerned in his somewhat arrogant look. Full of martial bonhomie and congratulation for themselves are the groups of civic guards at their banquets that Hals painted with an extraordinary skill, arranging them informally and yet in such a way as to give equal value to the individual portraits. The companies of civic guards had a distinguished place in municipal life and a history that long predated the fight for independence. The practice of commissioning a group portrait of the members started at Amsterdam in the early sixteenth century. Cornelis Anthonisz (*c.* 1499–1556) painted the city's civic guard in 1533, a formal and serious-looking assembly round the banquet

20. FRANS HALS. 'Malle Babbe' (Hille Bobbe). About 1630–33. Berlin-Dahlem, Staatliche Museen.

table (Amsterdam, Rijksmuseum). To compare this picture with the *Banquet of the Officers of the Company of St. George*, which Hals painted in 1627, is to realize freshly what vivacity he was able to impart to the scene.

Though Rembrandt (1606–69) belonged to the generation after Hals, as a young man he entered into the gay spirit of which older artists, Willem Buytewech (1591–1624), Hendrick Pot and Hals had given evidence. The laughing self-portraits (The Hague, Mauritshuis, and Amsterdam, Rijksmuseum) which Rembrandt painted when he was about 23 were much in Hals's vein. The portrait (Dresden), in which he raises his glass in cheerful toast while Saskia sits on his knee, was in the tradition of the 'merry companies' painted by various hands.

The fervour of patriotism had a powerful and long-sustained influence on Dutch art. It bred a sense of ownership which called for 'inventories' of the kind only a painter could then provide. Everything that most Dutch painters of the seventeenth century produced was a portrait of a sort. In addition to painting the likeness of their fellow countrymen and women, singly or in groups, artists depicted, with patriotic affection, their own flat lands instead of fanciful mountainous landscapes. Animals and birds were the special study of some; specialization was a general characteristic. There were still-life painters to satisy the pride of possession of the wealthy middle-class with pictures of the costly layout of their tables, the silver jugs and plates, the bowls of Chinese porcelain, the crystal goblets tinted with the rich translucence of the wine they hold. To tempt the appetite, still life arrayed an abundance of fruits, pies, hams, lobsters, oysters. . . . The flower painter gave his portraits the blooms of the garden, especially the tulip, first brought to Antwerp from Turkey and to the northern Netherlands from the south by refugees in the period of terror. One of them was Ambrosius Bosschaert (*c.* 1565–1621), a Protestant from Antwerp who introduced to Holland the Flemish style of flower painting practised by Jan Bruegel and others.

There were painters who specialized in townscapes and church interiors, and in depicting the spacious rooms, with tiled floors and Renaissance-style fireplaces, in which the rich took their ease. The marine painters celebrated the ships that were the main support of Holland's prosperity. The group portrait was almost a unique product of the northern provinces. It answered to a form of patronage that replaced the commission of altarpieces in the period before the religious schism and amounted to a public support for art. Though the officers of the civic guards each contributed to the amount paid for their group portrait, the companies were municipal institutions and thus the painting was in effect bought by the municipality.

A series of enormous canvases was commissioned between 1638 and 1643 at Amsterdam for the new hall of the *Kloveniers* (Musketeers), and included works by Jacob Backer (1608–1651), Nicolaes Elias (1588–*c.* 1655), Govert Flinck (*c.* 1615–60),

Bartholomeus van der Helst (1613–70) and, surpassing all the others, Rembrandt, with the wonderful painting familiar under the title of *The Night Watch* (Fig. 21), but more accurately described as *The Company of Frans Banning Cocq*. This great masterpiece of 1642, originally designed for the large hall of the *Kloveniersdoelen* was trimmed down, it is believed, when moved into a smaller room. The small copy (Fig. 22) made by Gerrit Lundens (1622–77) towards 1660, before the reduction in size, shows the painting to have then been even more majestic than now.

The vogue of the civic guard banquet came to a climactic end in 1648, when Van der Helst painted the vast canvas now in the Rijksmuseum for the Hall of the Long Bow Company at Amsterdam, showing their celebration of the Peace of Munster (Fig. 23), Govert Flinck and Gerard Terborch also producing works to mark the event. But the idea of the group portrait had been taken up by guilds, hospitals and charitable bodies such as had a board of governors, and remarkable examples continued to be produced in the second half of the century. Rembrandt's superb group of the officials of the Amsterdam cloth-makers' guild (*The Syndics*) was

21. REMBRANDT. The Night Watch. 1642. Amsterdam, Rijksmuseum.

painted in 1662, proof, incidentally, that *The Night Watch* was not as it was once supposed, unpopular enough to deprive Rembrandt of further important commissions.

At all times he had shown an ability to convey the shared interest of a group, the invisible thought-current that holds them together, as in *The Anatomy Lesson of Dr. Nicolaes Tulp*. It is a quality that distinguishes these works from the groups of Thomas de Keyser (1596/7–1667), Nicolaes Elias and Ferdinand Bol (1616–80) where each portrait seems without relation to the others. There was only Hals to match Rembrandt in the genre with that intense feeling of austere presence of *The Lady Governors of the Old Men's Home* (Haarlem, Frans Hals Museum), painted in 1664 towards the end of his life and in dramatic contrast with the debonair characters of his earlier *Banquets*.

Though the group portraits are to be accounted among Rembrandt's major works, he was in no way a specialist as the majority of his artist contemporaries were, except in so far as the study of humanity may be considered a specialization. His many portraits were not simply descriptive records of a man's features but profound psychological statements as well. The large number

22. GERRIT LUNDENS. Copy about 1660 of Rembrandt's 'The Night Watch' in its original dimensions. Amsterdam, Rijksmuseum. On loan from the National Gallery, London.

23. VAN DER HELST. The Banquet of the Civic Guard in Celebration of the Peace of Munster. 1648. Amsterdam, Rijksmuseum.

24. HONTHORST. Christ before the High Priest. About 1620. London, National Gallery.

of paintings and etchings he devoted to Biblical subjects was prompted by the range of human emotions contained in both Old and New Testaments, to which he could give visual interpretation.

Religious subjects as such were not popular in seventeenth-century Holland, though the Dutch painters who went abroad tended to adopt them from the masters whose style they studied in Italy. They were given a secularized form as scenes of ancient history rather than expressions of faith. There were two main influences on the Dutch painter in Italy: the German Adam Elsheimer (1578–1610), who long worked in Rome, and the great inventor, Caravaggio (1573–1610). Both gave light and shade a new value, Caravaggio especially in the dramatic oppositions that emphasized darkness, and were widely imitated in seventeenth-century Europe. The pupils of Abraham Bloemaert (1564–1651), himself an influential teacher and propagator of Italianate style, were prominent in bringing the 'tenebrism' of Caravaggio to Holland. Principal among them were Hendrick Terbrugghen (1588–1629), who settled at Utrecht after ten years in Italy, and Gerard van Honthorst (1590–1656), who also came back to Utrecht. Honthorst gave a plausible realism to Caravaggio-like exaggerations of light and shade by indicating an artificial source of illumination (Fig. 24)—candle, lamp or torch—for which he became known in Italy as 'Gherardo della Notte' ('Gerard of the Night').

Cornelis van Poelenburgh (c. 1586–1667) was also a pupil of Bloemaert who settled at Utrecht and followed Elsheimer in landscapes, introducing small figures of either Biblical or classical reference. Pieter Lastman (1583–1633), another Italianiser who spent some years in Rome, where he felt the influence of Elsheimer and Caravaggio, infused Caravaggism into 'history' pictures that are carried out in a narrative style without subtlety (Fig. 25). Lastman is of particular interest as the master (for six months) at Leiden of the young Rembrandt. Though he never went to Italy, the youthful Rembrandt was able to discern the significance of Caravaggio through its reflection in Honthorst and other Dutch followers. It was not only a trick of light and dark but an emphasis that brought out a basic humanity, the character of a Roman or Neapolitan proletariat, for which Rembrandt was to find a magnificent and more intellectual equivalent in the Jewish quarter of Amsterdam.

Though influenced by Caravaggio through the Utrecht painters and by Jacob Pynas (1585–1648) working in the style of Elsheimer, Rembrandt stands alone in the Dutch School of the seventeenth century in using darkness of tone not merely as the obstruction of light but as a substance to be moulded into effects of mystery and depth that stir the imagination. Realism in Dutch painting was on the whole differently orientated. The direct painting which seems to have been an original innovation by Frans Hals, using only four basic colours, black, white, yellow ochre and red, in touches laid down in almost Impressionist fashion, bears little resemblance to Rembrandt's technique. If black figures largely in seventeenth-century portraits this is often due to the fashion in dress, the black of wide-brimmed hat and other articles of costume providing the painter with the possibility of interesting silhouettes and, together with the lace of collar and cuffs, a kind of extra 'local colour'. When the flower painter used a black background this was a continuation of the Flemish practice intended simply to bring out the full brilliance of the blooms he depicted.

Realism in landscape necessarily gave prime importance to light. Hendrick Avercamp (1585–1634) could set a crowd of skaters against the background of pale wintry sky and frozen canal with an appreciation of the animated movement of the silhouetted figures that derived from Pieter Bruegel. Jan van Goyen (1595–1656) painted rivers and towns in Holland, first in a light monochrome and then with a delicate addition of colour that is full of atmosphere. Aelbert Cuyp (1620–91), termed with some appropriateness, 'the Dutch Claude', combined the Claudesque golden warmth of sky with the placidity of Dutch pastures and waterways.

The 'portrait' of Holland is completed by Meindert Hobbema (1638–1709), always with an eye for the picturesque qualities of a stretch of broken woodland, watermill or ancient farm but surpassing himself in that unique masterpiece, *The Avenue, Middelharnis*, in the National Gallery, London; and by the greatest of the Dutch specialists in landscape, Hobbema's master, Jacob van Ruisdael (1628/9–82).

His fresh and cloudy skies above the expanse of plain with, perhaps, a view of Haarlem gleaming in the far distance, were to be an inspiration to the young John Constable. His influence on the painters of Barbizon in nineteenth-century France was no less pronounced. That Rembrandt took as much pleasure as any in the character of his native land is conclusively shown by the number of drawings and etchings he made in the region around Amsterdam. With a few pen-strokes he evokes the canals, the windmills,

25. PIETER LASTMAN. Flight into Egypt. 1608. Rotterdam, Boymans-van Beuningen Museum.

39

26. NICHOLAS MAES. Dreaming. About 1655.
Amsterdam, Rijksmuseum.

the scattered cottages and farms, the spacious levels. In an
etching of about 1640, the city itself is a fascinating distant skyline
viewed from the edge of a winding dyke. Yet in his painted landscapes there is no link with those who portrayed the familiar and
well-recognizable scene. He invented a phantom land of heights
and ruins and shadowy spaces as full of mystery and depth as the
darkness from which, in his portraits, the countenances of his
sitters emerged.

The link here was with Hercules Seghers (1589/90–1637/8), the
independent forerunner whom Rembrandt admired and of whose
work he owned several examples. Seghers, born at Haarlem, was
the pupil of the Flemish landscape painter, Gillis van Coninxloo
(1544–1607), in the period when the latter was settled at
Amsterdam. He continued to paint imagined heights like those
that had resulted from the southward journeys of the Flemish
artists across the Alps to Italy. It is assumed that Seghers took
this route. The rocky slopes and desolate valleys he painted and
etched, though having a certain air of reality, possess a strangeness
also that no doubt appealed to the romantic side of Rembrandt's
nature.

27. CAREL FABRITIUS. Self-portrait. About 1650. Rotterdam, Boymans-van Beuningen Museum.

Rembrandt's pupils were mostly competent craftsmen in portraiture. Nicolas Maes (1634–93) was perhaps the most successful in following the master's style of domestic genre, a good example being the motif of a girl at a window in his *Dreaming* (Fig. 26) (Amsterdam, Rijksmuseum). When compared with Rembrandt's treatment of a similar subject (London, Dulwich College Gallery) it can be seen to lack Rembrandt's subtlety and depth of insight, though its charm is considerable. Carel Fabritius (1622–54), however, also a pupil, even when painting in Rembrandt's style as in the self-portrait in the Boymans-van Beuningen Museum (Fig. 27), reveals a decided originality still more decisively affirmed by his later reversing Rembrandt's practice of working from dark to light. The famous *Goldfinch* set in its perch against a light background (The Hague, Mauritshuis) is an example.

Fabritius, who settled at Delft, was probably the master of the

28. VERMEER. The Letter. About 1665.
Amsterdam, Rijksmuseum.

great Jan Vermeer (1632–75). The relation between the two would have been clearer if the explosion of the powder magazine at Delft in 1654, in which Fabritius was killed, had not at the same time destroyed most of his work. In his early paintings, influenced by Italy, there are bright hues rather than chiaroscuro. Vermeer is the magnificent opposite and complement to Rembrandt in light and colour.

In subject matter, much of the work of Vermeer continued the genre that marked the increasing refinement of Dutch society in the seventeenth century. In contrast with the vulgar jollity that Jan Steen (1626–79) still depicted, or the peasant scenes in which Adriaen van Ostade (1610–85) followed Brouwer, are the glimpses of well-appointed bourgeois interiors in which young women, whose good taste in reflected in dress of expensive simplicity, meditate over a letter, or play on the harpsichord or virginals. The tradition established by Jan Miense Molenaer (1610–88), Gerard Terborch (1617–81) and Gabriel Metsu (1629–67) was brought to perfection at Delft in the art of Vermeer.

In painting domestic scenes, exterior and interior, Pieter de Hooch (1629–81), during the period he worked at Delft, came near to Vermeer, but in colour and design the latter was the more creative spirit. Daylight as an influence on colour and colour as a system of calculated harmony were both new ideas in Dutch art. Concentrating on chiaroscuro, Rembrandt has used his deep reds and golden warmth of colour, primarily to enrich tone. Vermeer gives an independent value to the blue, so exquisite in his *The Letter* (Fig. 28) (Amsterdam, Rijksmuseum), with a lemon yellow as its foil and subtleties of grey and white, colour being altered in shadow rather than darkened. The abstract value of rectangles and geometrical progression has an equal part to play, even in scenes so realistic as his *Little Street* (Amsterdam, Rijksmuseum). Impeccable from a purely aesthetic standpoint, he distils the Dutch sense of calm, propriety and order, with a concentration no less intense than that which Rembrandt devotes to an essential humanity. Vermeer is assured of a place among the greatest European artists.

4. The Spanish Genius

IV. VELAZQUEZ. Portrait of Juan de Pareja.
1650. New York, Metropolitan Museum of Art.

The greatness of Spain in painting is found in a select few, among whom three artists ascend so far above their fellows that they tend to be seen in a kind of apotheosis and certainly at the very summit of European art. They are Domenicos Theotocopoulos, known as El Greco (1541?–1614), Diego Velazquez (1599–1660), and Francisco de Goya (1746–1828). Some similarity can be found between their eminence and that of Rembrandt in Holland and Rubens in the Spanish Netherlands, though not only had the Netherlands, north and south, a greater number of 'little masters' and more artists who displayed a large measure of originality at a distinguished level but also, speaking generally, a more consistent line of evolution.

It is possible to underrate such Spanish painters as Ribera and Zurbarán in comparison with the manifestly greater men, but the course of Spanish art is broken and hesitant apart from the tremendous affirmations of the few individuals. If one seeks for a root cause in early history it is necessary to go back to the period during which the greater part of the Iberian peninsula was under the rule of the Moslem invaders. The Moors at the time of the first Crusade, c. 1100 A.D., still occupied two-thirds of the land.

A gradual reconquest was made by the Christian regions, reclaiming the land bit by bit and planting churches and their visual message in one district after another. In Catalonia works still preserved in the museums of Barcelona convey the force of this active Christianity in paintings in a majestic Romanesque style. It was not until near the end of the fifteenth century that Spain was united as a country. The kingdoms of Castile and Aragon were conjoined in 1479 under Ferdinand and Isabella. The Moors were driven from their last foothold, Granada, in 1492. The long drawn-out struggle made the extension of painting a slow and uneven process. The province of Catalonia—the earliest to be freed from Moslem domination—had the advantage, in the Gothic period of the thirteenth and fourteenth centuries, of contacts with France and Italy, faintly reflected in the work of Ferrer Bassa (c. 1290–1348). In the Gothic churches of Spain, with the enlargement of windows at the expense of wall space which caused the atrophy of mural painting, huge altarpieces were produced with panels, painted in a style reminiscent of the Sienese school, by such artists as the brothers Pedro and Jaime Serra and Luis Borrassa (d. 1424).

The fifteenth century brought the influence of the great Netherlandish school, heralded by the visit of Jan van Eyck who, like Rubens at a later date, combined the function of diplomat with that of painter. The Flemish influence is seen to advantage in the painting of *St. Dominic of Silos* (Prado) by Bartolomé Bermejo, active 1474–95. But the contact with Renaissance Italy, so fruitful elsewhere, was limited. Pedro Berruguete (d. c. 1504) was an exception in working at Urbino at the same time as Piero della Francesca. His sense of form was quickened in that inspiring atmosphere, but he left Urbino after Duke Federigo's death in 1482 and the compromise—and some conflict—between the provincialized Flemish manner and the lessons of Umbria appears in his later work.

In the sixteenth century when Spain became a world power with vast possessions and sources of wealth in the New World as well as possessions dotted about Europe, it might have been expected that a vigorous national school of painting would come into being, transforming the somewhat tentative or imitative character that painting in Spain had shown up to then. It turned out otherwise. For the greater part of the century painting remained spiritless. Both the Emperor Charles V and his son Philip II of Spain were patrons with a feeling for art, but the great Venetians, especially Titian, claimed most of their interest. Philip also highly approved of the fantasies of Jerome Bosch—unaccountably to the churchmen who suspected heresy in these strange productions of the Netherlands.

Portraiture received a certain encouragement but it was Antonio Moro (as he was known in Spain), the Flemish practitioner of a style modelled on that of Titian, whom Philip II despatched to England to paint the portrait of Mary Tudor. Philip had two Spanish court painters, it is true: Alonso Sanchez Coello (c. 1531–88) who formed his style on that of Moro and his pupil, Juan Pantoja de la Cruz (1551–1608), who succeeded him. Dignified and with an element of ceremonial stiffness emphasized by the attention given to the rich detail of apparel, their portraits give some slight indication of what Velazquez would later achieve.

But the sixteenth century was not only the century of Spain's material splendour; it was also that of the great battle of religious beliefs in which she was heavily engaged under the rule of a monarch who was a relentless fanatic. A reason for this fanaticism and the cruelty and oppression it engendered may be found in the centuries-long struggle against the Moslems in Spain. The Spanish kings who had come to regard themselves as the champions and main bulwark of Christianity saw no more in the Protestant opposition to the Catholic Church than the action of infidels as bad as the Moors, to be combated with equal ruthlessness.

The fervour of religious belief had as yet found no strong expression in the images produced according to the Church's strict rules. There is no perceptible stir of deep emotion in the work of Luis de Morales (c. 1500–86), though its delicate piety, contained in a style adapted from Italianate Flemings perhaps working at Seville, earned him the title 'the divine'. But after *El Divino* Morales, there comes an extraordinary, an unpredictable phenomenon, the advent of El Greco; with him all the intensities of religious feeling in Spain take fire and burst into ecstatic flame.

It is a paradox that a painter who conveys so much that is essentially Spanish should have been a Cretan. And, furthermore, it is strange that one trained in the Byzantine style of the monks in this Greek island should have grafted onto it the High Renaissance lessons learned from Titian and Tintoretto in Venice. He could pass as a Venetian master when he came to Spain at about the age of 36. But by the work of his subsequent 37 years, spent mainly at Toledo, he becomes inseparable from the history of Spanish art.

In Toledo, the Spanish centre of the Counter-Reformation, seat of the dreaded Inquisition and of all the passionate intensities of belief, the paintings he produced in his vast studio lit by tall, narrow windows, became aspirations to the sublime, fevered exaltations of saints and martyrs, dramas of the soul expressed in the elongation of figures, the unquiet carmines, blue-greens and off-yellow of his colours. His masterpiece, *The Burial of Count Orgaz,* painted about 1586 for the church of Santo Tomé at Toledo, unites celestial movement and space—conceived like the *Paradise* of Tintoretto—with the static austerity of the mourners, a row of icons as one might imagine them, though each bearded visage has its own suggestion of an inward violence of feeling kept sternly under control (Fig. 29).

Though El Greco was successful and highly enough esteemed in his own day to be copied and imitated by his followers at Toledo,

29. EL GRECO. Detail from 'The Burial of Count Orgaz'. 1586. Toledo, Church of S. Tomé.

such as Luis Tristan (1586–1624) and others, a new phase of Spanish painting was at hand as also a new phase of Spanish history. The ascendancy of Spain was virtually at an end after the defeat of the Armada in 1588, the breakaway of the northern Netherlands and the death of Philip II in 1598. Philip III, his son by his third marriage, left government in the hands of the Duke of Lerma who, impressive as he appears in the equestrian portrait by Rubens now in the Prado, squandered public money and involved Spain in the futile misery of the Thirty Years' War.

Political and economic decadence can be a slow decline in the course of which art often attains its highest level, though there is no necessary relation between the two, except in the encouragement of art and letters by those more inclined to them than to politics. Spanish art in the seventeenth century reflects in its own

30. RIBERA. Archimedes. 1630. Madrid, Prado.

way a Europe-wide reaction against the Mannerism of the six-teenth century. A sense of reality that Mannerism had not offered, a projection of light and shade that delivered a message with an urgent force, was general. This was assimilated by Spanish artists to create a sombre magnificence in which a national mood may be discerned. The genius of the century inclined artists towards a realism or naturalism in religious compositions, substituting gnarled peasant models and proletarian types in the place of idealized figures, and unflinchingly depicting the tortures of martyrdom in gruesome detail. These are characteristics found in Italy in the work of Caravaggio whose influence was far-reaching. But Francisco Ribalta (1565–1628), born at Solsona in Catalonia—though associated mainly with Valencia—was already cultivating the tenebrist depth of shadow before Caravaggio embarked on his career.

Jusepe de Ribera (1591–1652) was of an age to appreciate both. He may have studied under Ribalta but by the time he was 25 had settled at Naples where he came to be regarded as the principal follower of Caravaggio. He worked for the Spanish viceroys at Naples and pictures by him were sent to Spain for the royal court. It was perhaps for this reason, and to affirm his patriotism, that he habitually added the name of his birthplace 'Jativa' or its neigh-bouring city 'Valencia', to his signature.

Ribera painted martyrdom with gloomy relish. Like Caravaggio he made a violent drama of the contrast between light and dense shadow. His realism was exercised not only on the tortures of religion but on everyday subjects in which the idea of suffering or deformity was present. An example is his painting of the lame and broken-toothed urchin in mock-military pose, the *Boy with a Club Foot* (Louvre), an outstanding work of his later years. Just as the realist repaired to the masses for the types to be included in a religious composition so Ribera seems to have selected a Neapolitan beggar to do duty for a great man of classical antiquity. The *Archimedes* (Fig. 30) of the Prado is a genial ruffian with a garment of many patches roughly tethered with string across his bare chest and, to judge by his expression, sharing the painter's ironical jest.

Absent though he was from Spain, Ribera was evidently a powerful influence, by virtue of his paintings, in disseminating the Caravaggesque style which is clearly to be distinguished from the rhapsodic emotionalism of the Baroque. An artist who comes near to greatness is Francisco Zurbarán (1598–1664). He worked as a boy in the studio of the Seville painter, Juan de las Roelas (c. 1560–1625), who brought a realistic tendency into painting at Seville in opposition to the then prevailing Mannerism borrowed from Rome. Zurbarán, settling in Seville, had an early success, churches and convents heaping commissions on him for paintings of religious theme. In middle-age, however, his popularity waned. The facile style of the young Esteban Murillo (1617–82) brought into vogue a sentimental religiosity, contrasting with his realistic genre (Fig. 31), to which Zurbarán could not adjust.

How original he was is a comparatively modern rediscovery.

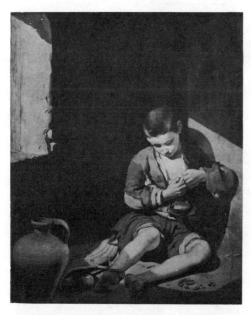

31. MURILLO. Beggar Boy. About 1645–55. Paris, Louvre.

The dark shadows of Ribera and the Neapolitan school helped him to picture the sombreness of monkish meditation. Unlike El Greco he painted the saint or friar engaged in meditation (Fig. 32) rather than celestial visions. He conveys the psychology of the devout, pondering on death according to Jesuit instruction. His realistic outlook also enabled him to paint still-life pictures in which the scrutiny of material substance has almost the intensity of a religious exercise.

It is against this background of Seville that Diego Rodriguez de Silva y Velazquez is first seen. There were a number of links with his contemporaries making for a realistic outlook. He shared the general enthusiasm for Caravaggio or at least for the implications of his style. His study of still life was as intense as that of the

32. ZURBARÁN. St. Francis in Meditation. About 1635–8. London, National Gallery.

friend of his youth, Zurbarán. Every corrugation on the jug of his *Water Seller* (London, Wellington Museum), is traced out with as much care as the portraitist might give to the wrinkles of a human face.

In Ribera's fashion he bestowed on the contemporary characters he painted the names of ancient celebrities—the philosopher Menippus, the fabulist Aesop (Fig. 33). Nor did he hesitate to portray the sad grotesques and dwarfs of Philip IV's court as realistically as Ribera painted the club-footed boy. The *bodegones* or 'kitchen pictures' of his early years at Seville place him close to Caravaggio and his early religious pictures are parallel with those of Zurbarán; but after a certain point he ceases to resemble others and becomes entirely individual in style.

Religious subjects ceased to occupy him (not perhaps entirely to the regret of a realist absorbed in human affairs) after he had been appointed court painter to Philip IV. Portraiture then became his main professional task yet he shows a surprising diversity of theme. He was unique among painters in religious Spain in taking up mythological subjects though, as Rembrandt did, with an anti-idealist sentiment. The first of his compositions to attract court notice was the *Triumph of Bacchus* otherwise known as *The Topers*. The classical allusion, however, was no more than a pretext for as vivid a picture as has ever been painted of a group of intensely Spanish peasants.

Mythology sanctioned the painting of the nude figure—a rarity in Spanish art except for the drooping and tortured form of Christ on the Cross. *The Forge of Vulcan* and *Mars* were subjects enabling Velazquez to do justice to the male figure, but more purely delightful is *The Toilet of Venus*, as little mythological as Rembrandt's *Danae*. The mystery of space and the relation of objects occupied him in *The Maids of Honour (Las Meniñas)* where the painter at his large canvas gazes into the room at himself painting at his canvas, while the king and queen looking over his shoulder are reflected in the mirror at the opposite end of the room. An intricate theme is likewise developed in the varied action of *The Tapestry Weavers*. Among the greatest ..istorical compositions is *Las Lanzas* depicting one of the ephemeral victories of Spain in her losing battle against the rebel provinces of the Netherlands and showing Justin of Nassau handing over the keys of the city to the Spanish commander Spinola in 1625. Painted some ten years after the event the picture is famous not only for its design but for the friendly exchange of courtesies expressed in the bearing of victor and vanquished in which something of Velazquez' own magnanimity of mind may have coloured the rendering of the event. It was a magnanimity he displayed with equal courtesy to his sitters whether a court dwarf, an idiot jester, an Infanta, or the melancholy king himself.

Velazquez could meet Rubens in person and could study the works of the Renaissance masters during his two visits to Italy without in the least departing from a way of painting entirely his own. In his mature works it is no longer the darkness of shadow

33. VELAZQUEZ. Aesop. About 1638–41. Madrid, Prado.

that strikes the observer but colour used with infinite address in sparkling touches offset by silvery grey. What was simply the imitation of pattern in some rich article of dress in the portraits of Sanchez Coello, becomes a chromatic vibration of blues, pinks and greys in Velazquez' portraits of Philip IV's second wife, Mariana of Austria, and the Infanta Margarita. In these and in his two small views of the gardens of the Villa Medici, which resulted from his second visit to Italy, he gives a suggestion of what was later to become the method of Impressionism.

Velazquez left behind no considerable influence on Spanish painting. His pupil and son-in-law Juan Bautista del Mazo (c. 1612/16–67) copied him in a superficial way which has in the past caused some misattributions to Velazquez himself. Juan Pareja (c. 1606–70), Velazquez' servant, also imitated him. But Spanish art passed through another fallow period in the eighteenth century, though for a while a measure of prosperity returned to the country during the peaceful reaction from wars in which one possession after another had been lost.

The court painters of Philip V (1683–1746), first Bourbon king of Spain, were French (Ranc, Houasse, Van Loo). His son Ferdinand VI (1713–59) favoured Italian painters (Amiconi, Giaquinto). There was long a dearth of native talent except for Luis Melendez (1716–80) who ably continued the Spanish still-life tradition of Zurbarán and Sanchez Cotan (1561–1627). Then again comes the extraordinary, the unpredictable phenomenon, in Francisco de Goya (1746–1828).

Spain in Goya's time suffered drastic changes of fortune. The benevolent despotism of Charles III, who succeeded Ferdinand VI and ruled from 1759 to 1788, brought about economic stability. The folly of Charles IV, Charles III's successor, put an end to prosperity and opened the way to the Napoleonic invasion and its attendant horrors. On a wider scale, change from before the French Revolution to the period following affected all Europe. No great artist passed through this time of disturbance without in some way reflecting its storms and stress. Of this Goya gives dramatic illustration.

El Greco was the artist of the Church and Velazquez of the Court. Goya was distinct from both in being the artist of the People. There is a remarkable contrast between him and Velazquez. The latter was essentially the great gentleman, like Rubens, leading a life of aristocratic calm in the Escorial, painting in the cool twilight of a room screened from the blaze of sun outside, unruffled by events in the outer world and perhaps the more detached from the national concerns of Spain by being the son of a Portuguese father. Goya, the son of a small-town Spanish craftsman, Josef Goya, master gilder at Fuentetodos in Aragon, had a varied experience and was so responsive to events that his work is a whole history of an epoch of violence. The last fling of the rococo gaiety of the Old Regime is mirrored in the paintings, designed to be copied in tapestry, depicting scenes of Spanish life and diversions with a touch of Tiepolo's decorative and theatrical style. But the French Revolution made him critical of court and clergy and though in middle-age he was court painter, first to Charles III and then to Charles IV, there remained a revolutionary current in his thought, cryptically expressed in his graphic work. Embittered by the deafness that followed an illness in his fifties, he felt the more keenly the savagery of war and occupation of which he has given his immortal testimony. As Charles IV and his son Ferdinand virtually invited the French to take over by submitting their quarrels to Napoleon's arbitration it is hardly to be wondered at that Napoleon should have supplanted both with his own family candidate, Joseph, or that Goya's portraits of them should give the impression of an imbecility mercilessly caricatured.

'Rembrandt, Velazquez and Nature' was Goya's own summing up of the sources of his inspiration. A reminiscence of Rembrandt's chiaroscuro may be found in the shadows of his *Prison Scene*; the influence of Velazquez in the exquisite greys of the posthumous portrait (Prado) of his brother-in-law, the painter Francisco Bayeu. In his painting of the loins and sheep's head of a butcher's counter, Goya chose as unconventional a still-life subject as Rembrandt's *Slaughtered Ox*.

His devotion to 'nature' may be taken to refer to his interest in human life in all its aspects rather than to landscape, but 'nature' had also a special meaning for him. The objects we see, he pointed out, have no fixed outlines. By dispensing with outline in his paintings he anticipated a cardinal point of Impressionist technique. In other ways he had an affinity with or influence on nineteenth-century French art. The eerie, dark groups he painted in his later years with the strangeness of expression that his deafness may have caused him to dwell on, link him with Daumier. The *Third of May, 1808* incited Manet to paint the execution of the Emperor Maximilian in a similar composition. In comparison Goya has the advantage of conveying a shock directly felt instead of having, like Manet, to imagine an historical event from a far distance.

In the nineteenth century, after Goya, art in Spain was once more a fallow field but in this century there has again been a sudden extraordinary development after a long interval, this time in an international context. The history of a period of violence unfolds in the work of Picasso as in that of Goya.

5. The Development of Portraiture

V. TITIAN. Pope Paul III and his grandsons.
1546. Naples, Museo di Capodimonte.

There are many portraits among the masterpieces of European painting from the fifteenth century to recent times and they are an important feature of the work of masters who excelled in other genres. Goya, the painter of Spanish life, of the bull-fight, of popular festival, of sinister omen, of the disasters of war, even of religious subjects would yet be incomplete in our view without his brilliant studies of the individual personality.

For the greater part of the medieval period, in an art dedicated to religion, such studies (had it been possible to make them) would have seemed an intrusion on the ground belonging to faith, an impertinence if nothing more. The sculptured effigies of kings and queens were memorial abstractions of authority. Manuscript illumination provided symbols rather than likenesses, until the later Middle Ages. The beginnings of characterization appear in royal portraits of the fourteenth century, the Wilton Diptych providing an example. Yet, beautiful work as it is in a delicate miniature style, seemingly related to that of the Franco-Flemish artist André Beauneveu, it poses a problem in the image it gives of the young and beardless Richard II. There is some evidence to show that the panel was painted at a later date when Richard was bearded and prematurely aged. Whatever the reason, this would imply that likeness was not such a primary concern as attitude and devotional content.

In Flemish painting of the fifteenth century the realistic portrait comes into being with a startling suddenness. The practice of including the likeness of the donor—prelate, noble or wealthy merchant—in the altarpiece destined for church or convent exercised the superb skills of Jan van Eyck, Roger van der Weyden and Hans Memlinc. They painted purely secular portraits with the same power, foreign visitors to the Flemish cities being among their clients. The agent of the Medici at Bruges, Tommaso Portinari, appears with his wife and children in the great *Adoration*, now in the Uffizi, by Hugo van der Goes. Sir John Donne, knighted by Edward IV during the Wars of the Roses, was portrayed with his wife and daughter in the triptych by Hans Memlinc (1477), now in the National Gallery, London, (Fig. 34). An Englishman abroad, Edward Grimston of Rishangles, Suffolk, had earlier been the subject of a purely secular painting by Petrus Christus, the follower of Van Eyck at Bruges. The fellow-feeling between England and the southern Netherlands thus extended to art was to have a sequel in the long succession of Flemish painters settling in London in the sixteenth and seventeenth centuries.

Humanism, the Renaissance and the Reformation all contributed to the development of portraiture as an independent genre. The principle of the humanist philosophy—that the proper study of mankind was man—logically gave the portrait a place of importance. The artists of the Renaissance were not only in accord with this view but by technical advance they improved the representation of character. The oil medium brought to Venice by Antonello da Messina gave a new warmth and strength of

34. HANS MEMLINC. Detail of donor from the 'Donne' Triptych. About 1477. London, National Gallery.

57

modelling to the art. Leonardo (1452–1519) demonstrated how light and shade could add to the suggestion of personality and psychology. The Reformation gave an impetus to portraiture of another kind. The suppression of religious imagery in the reforming lands made painters the readier to offer their services as portraitists.

The career of Hans Holbein the Younger (1497–1543) shows the effect of the three forces. Born at Augsburg, he chose to work when young in the German-Swiss city of Basle which as well as being prosperous was a centre of scholarly humanism. It was there he made his illustrations for the *Praise of Folly* by Erasmus. He had the Renaissance capacity for varied undertakings, from mural decoration and altarpieces to designs for goldsmith's work and stained glass, though his bent towards portraiture was already marked. But in the upsurge of Protestant feeling at Basle, employment of a Catholic nature came to an end.

Like other artists he was 'without bread', as Erasmus observed in recommending him to Thomas More in London. The interest of these friends (which he repaid by superb portraits of them) enabled Holbein to meet and portray in paintings and drawings a considerable sector of Tudor society in the two years of his first stay in England, 1526–8. His second stay of eleven years from 1532 to his death in 1543 brought him more definitely into the court sphere. He became painter to Henry VIII in 1536. No face in history is better known than the formidable visage with suspicious eyes and small cruel mouth painted by Holbein in the one picture (Thyssen Collection)—among a number of versions—that is certainly from his own hand.

In this century of shifting relations and alliances between despotic rulers the portrait had its diplomatic function. Besides providing a reminder at home to officials and courtiers of the governing power, the ruler-image was a symbol of international exchange, the artist himself an international figure. This was the position of Titian, the portrayer of Charles V and Philip II of Spain: and of Anthonis Mor van Dashorst, the Latin 'Antonio Moro', who later became Sir Anthony More and painted Mary Tudor and Sir Thomas Gresham.

Before photography was invented—or personal acquaintance considered a necessary preliminary even to a royal marriage—the painted portrait served to convey the physical suitability of the prospective bride. Holbein was despatched to the continent to bring back his pictorial report on the young but widowed Duchess of Milan and Anne, daughter of the Duke of Cleves, to assist Henry in making his choice. More than a description, his painting of the Duchess (London, National Gallery) became a masterpiece adding to the attraction of feature a splendid simplicity of design (Fig. 35).

Another purpose of the court portrait was to indicate power and rank by the splendour of costume and profusion of jewellery. This was strongly characteristic of the Elizabethan period, and perhaps a requirement of the patron that features should have a stiff and

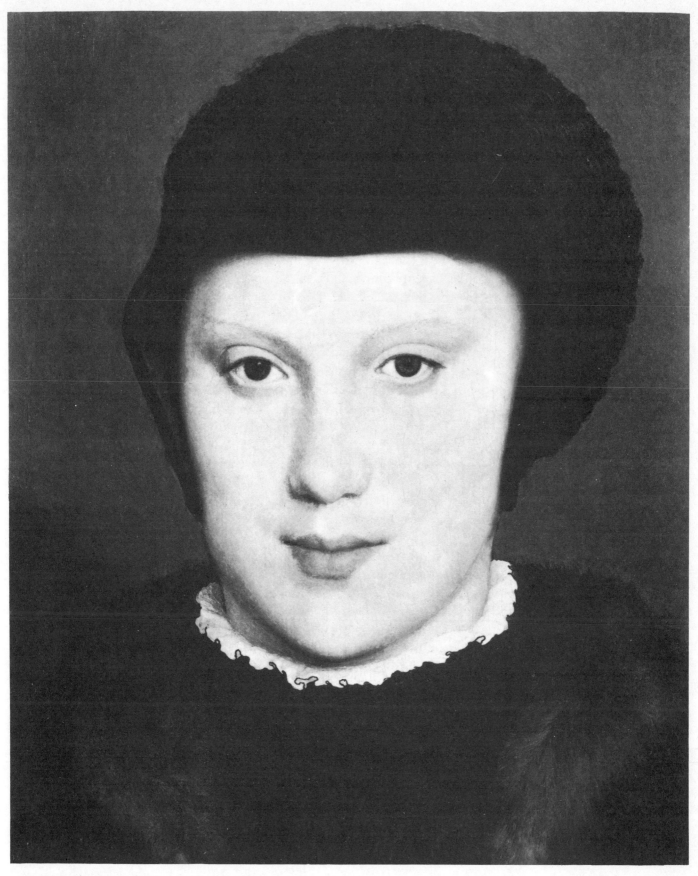

35. HOLBEIN THE YOUNGER. Detail. Christina
of Denmark, Duchess of Milan. 1538. London,
National Gallery.

36. VAN DYCK. Queen Henrietta Maria, wife of Charles I. 1638–9. Windsor Castle, Royal Collection. By gracious permission of Her Majesty the Queen.

37. SAMUEL COOPER. Barbara Villiers, Duchess of Cleveland. 1661. Windsor Castle, Royal Collection. By gracious permission of Her Majesty the Queen.

ceremonially expressionless aspect while the wealth of accessories gave evidence of status. The queen herself seems to have thought along these lines in her injunctions against shadow conveyed to Nicholas Hilliard, against, that is, the facial modelling shadow would produce.

The almost Byzantine formal richness of such a work as the *Ditchley Portrait* by Marcus Gheeraerts the Younger was sought by court ladies in their lesser degree. The Flemish painters who came to England to escape religious persecution in the Netherlands and formed a Flemish colony in London were craftsmen supplying a requirement which limited their independence as artists. The miniature by its intimate scale avoided the heaviness of restriction —the art of Hilliard in its clarity of colour, vivacity of delineation and emblematic poetry coming to the eye as melodiously as the Elizabethan sonnet to the ear.

The seventeenth century was a great age of portraiture in Europe. The status of the painter was altered, he could claim a greater degree of independence in method and conception. The respect in which Titian had been held by the most powerful of rulers had left an abiding impression. The artist moved in court circles not as a hired workman but as one who added to their lustre. Where no court existed—in the united provinces of the northern Netherlands—newly gained wealth and national freedom called for portraits in plenty. It has been said that every Flemish artist was a born portrait painter and to survey the course of Flemish painting from Van Eyck to Rubens and Van Dyck is to realize how much truth there is in this observation.

Even so, the portraiture of Renaissance Italy had set a standard by which the seventeenth century profited. Raphael's portrait of Baldassare Castiglione which Rembrandt saw at Amsterdam suggested the style of composition he adopted in the self-portrait of 1640 (London, National Gallery). The eight years spent by Rubens in Italy in the service of the Duke of Mantua, when he copied the great Venetians for the Duke and also for his own satisfaction, were years in which his originality was fostered by Italian example. In Van Dyck's six years in Italy, painting portraits and studying the Venetians, he derived much from the dignity of pose and rich colour of Titian.

Van Dyck can be viewed in two distinct aspects. There is the Baroque painter of emotional religious compositions that vie with those of Rubens in the churches of Antwerp, and there is the portrait painter more sensitive to psychological atmospheres than his master, Rubens. The coolness and restraint of England exerted their influence. The elegance and refinement of Van Dyck's art (Fig. 36) dominated the century in England though William Dobson (1610–46) arrived independently at a vigorous style based on study of the Venetians, and Samuel Cooper (1609–72) stands out as one who could exquisitely reduce the effect of a large oil portrait to miniature scale (Fig. 37). The decline of a 'court art' can be traced in the work of Sir Peter Lely (1618–80) and Sir Godfrey Kneller (1646–1723). A race of aristocratic Parliamentar-

38. FRANCIS HAYMAN. Hambleton Custance
and Thomas Nuthall(?). About 1750. Banbury,
Upton House, National Trust (Bearsted
Collection).

ians and country gentlemen were the patrons in the period of
England's greatest excellence in the portrait, the eighteenth
century.

An informality and intimacy that Europe had not known appear
in the portraits of the age. The 'conversation pieces' practised by a
number of artists—William Hogarth (1697–1764) foremost among
them—give an example (Fig. 38). Consisting of a family group or
group of friends, they differed from such groups in Dutch or
French art by showing the subjects informally engaged in some

39. GAINSBOROUGH. John Plampin of Chadacre. About 1750–55. London, National Gallery.

40. REYNOLDS. Self-portrait. About 1773. London, Royal Academy.

customary occupation or diversion in their usual surroundings. The pleasures of owning a country property are suggested by the portraits in open-air setting painted by Thomas Gainsborough (Fig. 39) (1727–88). The freshness of English beauty made its wholesome contrast with the elaborate make-up of the court ladies of old, while children were no longer portrayed as small effigies encased in ceremonial dress but in natural movement and expression.

Instead of courtiers, a wide range of types and character appears. Hogarth for preference paints the middle-class philanthropist Captain Coram or a group of his own servants. Sir Joshua Reynolds (1723–92) paints the actor, the actress, the man of letters—Garrick, Mrs. Siddons, Dr. Johnson—as well as lords and ladies. George Stubbs (1724–1806) and others paint the sporting squires out hunting or shooting.

There were still strong links with the past in the eighteenth century. Gainsborough came to the point when he rediscovered Van Dyck and refashioned the Flemish master's elegance in English style. Reynolds (Fig. 40) gave his learned pictorial commentary on Rembrandt and Titian. The nineteenth century, less secure of its moorings, was more fitful and varied in style in the portraits that can be considered as works of art—leaving aside the large accumulation of works of an undistinguished and quasi-photographic character, product of growing population and middle-class wealth. The eighteenth-century tradition disappears in the temperamentally romantic brilliance of Sir Thomas Lawrence (1769–1830). The Victorian Age presents such variations as the early portraits of Sir John Millais (1829–96) with their astonishing Pre-Raphaelite minuteness; the portraits of George Frederick Watts (1817–1904) which with some idealization well represent the intense earnestness of the Great Victorians; and the aesthetic conception of James McNeill Whistler (1824–1903) who viewed the portrait as an 'arrangement' of colours and shapes, rather than as a revelation of character.

Twentieth-century painters have been somewhat oppressed by the idea that photography has made the painted portrait superfluous but there are examples to show that this need little concern the artist of originality. There are many who have pondered the enigma presented by their own features with original result. The combination of a painter's individuality of style, the personality of the sitter and the suggestion of a particular type of society has still remained beyond the camera's imitation.

6. The Development of Landscape

Britain now seems so essentially a home of landscape painting, especially when one thinks of the superlative powers of John Constable (1776–1837) and Joseph Mallord William Turner (1775–1851) that it is surprising to recall the opinion expressed by Horace Walpole in his *Anecdotes of Painting* concerning the country's backwardness in the art. In that work, published in 1761, he remarked in somewhat cool reference to one of the English pioneers of landscape, George Lambert (*c.* 1700–65): 'In a country so profusely beautified with the amenities of nature it is extraordinary that we have produced so few good painters of landscape . . .'

Walpole deprecated the practice of painting 'precipices and castellated mountains because Virgil gasped for breath at Naples and Salvator wandered amidst Alps and Apennines', complaining that 'our ever verdant lawns, rich vales, fields of haycocks and hop-grounds are neglected as homely and familiar subjects'. The remark was not entirely justified. Gainsborough had painted his *Cornard Wood* and *View of Dedham* (Fig. 41) a long time before Walpole wrote. A topographical tradition already existed in the first half of the century. Samuel Scott (*c.* 1702–72) began to paint his views of London and the Thames in the 1730s, a decade before Canaletto (1697–1768) came to the city to exchange for a while the Grand Canal at Venice for the river at Westminster.

It is true, however, that the second half of the century was the more fruitful and that it took time for the connoisseurs of the period to get used to the notion that artists in Britain had an original contribution to make. The European traditions of the north and south were both admired though for different reasons. The 'classical' landscape that had grown up in Italy had its irresistible appeal for the cultured islander on the Grand Tour. 'Classical' is an ambiguous word but it serves to suggest the respect

41. GAINSBOROUGH. View of Dedham. About 1750. London, Tate Gallery.

for antiquity that was especially strong in artists who had come to Italy from Northern Europe, manifest in their paintings of Roman ruins and regions to which there was classical reference. Paul Bril, Adam Elsheimer and the Bolognese painters Annibale Carracci (1560–1609) and Domenichino (1581–1641) added to elaborately decorative arrangements of trees and lakes the suggestion of classical subject in the small figures they introduced. Yet another implication of the word 'classical' may be found in the sense of order and measure conveyed by the landscapes of Nicolas Poussin (1594–1665).

It is evident that there was much poetic and romantic feeling in this kind of landscape, delightfully rendered in the landscapes of Claude Lorrain (1600–82), who combined dream-like visions of an ancient past with beautifully observed effects of dawn and sunset. Poetry of another kind was to be found in the wild and rugged scenes inspired by Calabria that were painted by Salvator Rosa (1615–73). Claude, Poussin and Salvator were venerated names to English connoisseurs of the eighteenth century. Also much admired was Gaspard Dughet (1615–75), Nicolas Poussin's brother-in-law and admirable pupil, who adopted the name 'Poussin'. But Claude in particular was the British idol; his carefully irregular disposition of trees and architectural features being copied by the cultivated owners of estates and their gardeners in actual trees, stretches of water and classical accessories: English parkland interpreted Claude in three dimensions.

The other tradition was that of Netherlandish painting in its more domestic aspect. Pride of possession mingled with feelings of affection. For Rubens the region round his own country house, the Château de Steen, near Malines, had a personal interest, leading him to paint every detail with loving care. The Dutch painters of the seventeenth century had their patriotic attachment to the land that had been wrested from foreign domination. The levels seamed with waterways, the horizontals picturesquely broken here and there by windmills and patches of woodland, the whole low-lying scene canopied by the moving panorama of cloud were as intimate and homely as the Arcadia of the painters in Rome was idealized fancy and the Calabria of Salvator romantically savage.

There were connoisseurs in England as devoted to the Dutch school of landscape as to the classical, to Jacob van Ruisdael and Meindert Hobbema as to Claude and Poussin. A certain geographical similarity between Holland and the East Anglian counties may account in part for the number of Dutch pictures acquired by those families of wealth with houses in the region. English landscapists were for a long time treated with less respect. A George Lambert might be employed to portray a mansion in the same way as a minor portrait painter might be called in to paint a member of the family but a Lambert's imitation of Gaspard could obviously not be treated with the same respect as the work of Dughet himself.

The beautiful pictures of Suffolk landscape painted by Gainsborough in his early years were a phase of his art that faded away in the compulsion that caused him to move to Bath and become a fashionable portrait painter. The landscape of his later years— a townsman's escape—had no sense of locality, though it had the corresponding advantage of light and mass in themselves.

The career of Richard Wilson (1714–82) is an instance of the ill-success of a greatly gifted artist who could only superficially be regarded as an imitator of the masters of classical landscape in Italy. Wilson did well enough as a portrait painter until at the age of 36 he went to Italy. He worked at Rome and Naples, where he had several pupils and was encouraged to concentrate on land-scape by fellow artists such as Francesco Zuccarelli (1704–88), the painter of decorative pastorals. Returning to London after six years, professedly as a landscape painter, he found that the qualities of breadth and simplicity which made his glowing Italian landscapes truly original (Fig. 42) were disregarded by

42. RICHARD WILSON. Ruins of the 'Villa of Maecenas', Tivoli. About 1755. London, Tate Gallery.

those who wished for more glamorous souvenirs of classical ground.

The connoisseurs no doubt took the view of Sir Joshua Reynolds that Wilson's landscapes were 'too near common nature' to admit the inclusion of gods and goddesses. The mythological flavouring was what they valued. It was the next generation—and more especially the next generation of artists—that was to appreciate Wilson's greatness.

Born within a year of each other, Constable and Turner were equally responsive to the outstanding masters of the tradition outlined above. What remains of Constable's lectures on landscape painting shows in what proportion he saw the past. It was a spectacle of greatness, decline and revival. He passed in eulogistic review, the merits of Poussin 'tranquil, penetrating and studious', 'the lofty energy' of the Caracci, the 'sentiment and romantic grandeur' of Domenichino, the 'serene beauty' of the 'inimitable' Claude, the 'wild and terrific' conceptions of Salvator Rosa, the 'freshness and dewy light' of Rubens who 'delighted in phenomena'.

For Constable, Rembrandt's *Mill* was an epoch in itself though he did not omit praise of Ruisdael and Cuyp. The decline was that of men who 'had lost sight of nature', among them Boucher whose 'scenery', said Constable, was 'a bewildered dream of the picturesque'. He had little good to say of John Wootton (*c.* 1686–1765) or George Lambert. From these depths, landscape painting was rescued by Wilson and Gainsborough to whose names Constable, recognizing no distinction of merit between oil

43. THOMAS GIRTIN. Kirkstall Abbey, Yorkshire. 1800. London, Victoria & Albert Museum.

painting and watercolour, added those of the watercolourists J. R. Cozens (1752–97/9) and Thomas Girtin (Fig. 43) (1775–1802).

If Turner had likewise set out what he valued in the past his selection of masters would not have differed greatly from Constable's. He studied Claude as intently as Constable studied the works by him in Sir George Beaumont's collection. He would have concurred in giving an honourable place to the watercolourists alongside the oil painters. Had he not worked with Girtin at Dr. Monro's and admired Cozens (Fig. 44) when copying his finely austere Alpine views (Fig. 45)?

Constable and Turner may be considered alike not only in their view of the landscape tradition but in reflecting consciously or unconsciously the idea of a return to nature so much in the air as

44. J. R. Cozens. Alpine Scenery. 1776. London, Victoria & Albert Museum.

45. J. M. W. Turner. Source of the Arveyron. 1802–3. Mr. & Mrs. Paul Mellon Collection.

46. JOHN CROME. Mousehold Heath, Norwich. About 1818. London, Victoria & Albert Museum.

the end of the century approached and its earlier urbanities and conventions palled. Jean-Jacques Rousseau had advanced the idea philosophically, and even Boucher's 'pastoral of the Opera house', as Constable contemptuously described it, indicates the half-serious though also frivolous way in which the French court was impressed. Wordsworth gave the idea poetical exposition in England, with his preface on the principles of poetry in the 1800 edition of the *Lyrical Ballads*. However, the poetic feeling for nature had been gaining impetus since James Thompson had published his collected *The Seasons* fifty years before. How his descriptions of landscape stimulated Turner is made evident by the quotations appended to the titles of his pictures in the Royal Academy catalogues.

In spite of their equal regard for nature and many points of similarity in taste it is surprising to realize what a vast difference there was between the two nearly contemporary painters. Constable, the countryman born, was an artist of local attachments, to his native Suffolk, to the flat lands and their great arch of sky in preference to the mountains that stirred the romantic imagination; and he had no wish to go outside England for theme or stimulus.

East Anglia had a special capacity for holding the affections of artists born in the region. John Crome (1768–1821), who spent nearly the whole of his life in his native city of Norwich and as the

47. CONSTABLE. Barge on the Stour. About
1811. London, Victoria & Albert Museum.

founder of the Norwich Society of Artists in 1803 became the
leader of England's only local school, was even more of a regional-
ist than Constable (Fig. 46). Unlike either, Turner, born in west
central London, amid dusky brick and under smoke-laden sky had
to travel to gain his first experience of rural landscape. The
topographical drawing which brought him early success caused
him to make frequent expeditions about the country, and the
romantic restlessness as well as the demand for albums with
illustrations of places abroad, which arose at the end of the
Napoleonic wars, impelled him regularly about Europe.

As a romantic he may be contrasted with Constable, the realist.
The latter habitually worked direct from nature in oil-sketches
and studies designed to capture as authentically and spontaneously
as possible the light and atmosphere of the scene before him (Fig.
47). The romanticism of Turner read into the Claudesque accessories of ancient ruins the whole tragedy of the decline and fall of
civilizations and exulted in the foaming torrents and vertiginous
chasms of Alpine routes. Constable was content with placid
canals and smiling cornfields; Turner destroyed reality in order to

extract from it a new release of energies, of chromatic vibrations. Constable came to the seaside at Brighton for the benefit of sea air for his ailing wife and marvellously conveyed the freshness of the atmosphere. Turner had to cross the sea, his favoured element, to experience and convey its power and rage.

Neither of these two supreme masters of landscape had any immediate influence in their own country though the electric shock of truth was immediately felt in France when *The Hay Wain* was shown in Paris. Its acclaim was, said Constable (with a notable absence of that respect which other insular painters have shown for the French), due to the fact that vivacity and freshness were 'things unknown to their own pictures . . . they neglect the look of nature altogether, under its various changes'. Any short-coming in this respect was to be made good by the Impressionists —whom Constable certainly anticipated—in the second half of the nineteenth century. Turner's conjunction of the elements was a more revolutionary adventure. The expressionist and abstract art of recent times, if not directly influenced by him, can at least refer to his great example and point to the fact that he called in a new world of art to redress the balance of the old.

7. *Realism to Impressionism*

VII. Courbet. Detail from 'L'Atelier'. 1854–55.
Paris, Louvre.

Edouard Manet (1832–83) and Pierre Auguste Renoir (1841–1919) are two great French artists round whom and through whose work there flow the intermingled currents of Realism and Impressionism. These related movements arose out of an understandable reaction against the formulas of painting that were influential in France in the first half of the nineteenth century. There was the formula of Romanticism, a term that came into use in the 1830s and was applied to the art of Eugène Delacroix (1798–1863), though not welcomed by him. In his painting the romantic element of subject matter drawn from the past was infused with intensities of feeling and colour in a way that produced a vital work of art.

In other hands this historical subject matter deteriorated into historical anecdote. Paul Delaroche (1797–1856) gives an example in such works as *The Princes in the Tower* (Louvre). Opposed to Romanticism was the Classicism upheld by Ingres (1780–1867) but this too involved a return to the past in subject matter and created another form of the official art of the Salons. An example is the admixture of anecdote and nudity sanctioned by antique setting that appears in the work of Léon Gérôme (1824–1904).

The pictures of Delaroche, Gérôme and others like them were popular with a middle-class society which enjoyed the glimpses they afforded of historical glamour and event (however much falsified) and had little concern with what was good as painting. These pictures were an escape from what many considered the drabness of bourgeois life in the post-revolutionary epoch. Their producers were zealous to present the profitable métier as a form of idealism that maintained lofty standards in art; and equally so in decrying, or as far as they could, in excluding from exhibition, works by those who might seek to establish other and opposite standards.

This was the situation when in the 1840s Gustave Courbet (1819–77) came forward as the champion of Realism. Classicism and Romanticism as he saw these movements were two aspects of the same falsity. It resulted from not looking at 'real and existing things'. The remedy was 'to interpret the manners, ideas and aspect of our own time'. This could best be achieved he thought in works taken from the common level of existence. The peasants and local characters he knew at his birthplace, Ornans, are seen in sombre verisimilitude in the *Burial at Ornans* (Louvre), a controversial exhibit in the Salon of 1850.

Thus began a long battle between the official rulers of the Salon and an unsympathetic press and public on the one side and the artists of original character on the other. The rejection of the *Burial* and also of Courbet's masterpiece, *L'Atelier*, by the jury of the Universal Exhibition of 1855 caused the undaunted rebel to stage the defiant exhibition of his own, with a catalogue containing his Realist manifesto, which placed the aims and the issue fairly and squarely before the art world.

Courbet's tough and commanding personality as well as the force of his work overcame opposition in the 1860s but by that time another victim had been singled out for persecution—Edouard Manet. The rejection of the first picture he submitted to the Salon, the *Buveur d'Absinthe* of 1859, initiated a series of refusals and humiliations reaching their most notorious point with *Le Bain* (later and better known as *Le Déjeuner sur l'Herbe*) and *Olympe*, the scandal of the Salon in 1865.

It may be questioned why Manet should have incurred far more hatred than Courbet seeing that he was much less provocative in statement, wishing as he said simply to paint in his own way without the least intention of overturning other existing methods of painting. It was his ambition to appear in the Salon alongside its most conventional adherents.

Yet he was a revolutionary in spite of himself. Like Courbet, Manet aimed at being contemporary in his art. He went farther than Courbet in being contemporary not only in subject but in style (Fig. 48). Ostensibly the offence of the *Déjeuner sur l'Herbe* was against propriety, in showing a naked young woman at an *al fresco* picnic with fully-dressed young men. But the comments of critics at the time suggest that they suffered optically rather than morally, from the unfamiliar manner rather than the matter of Manet's works.

Manet looked back first to the realism of seventeenth-century Holland, as represented by Frans Hals, and of Spain as represented by Velazquez and Goya. The direct painting of Frans Hals in particular suggested a crisp simplification of tone and colour

48. MANET. La Musique aux Tuileries. 1862. London, National Gallery.

49. COROT. Pont de Narni. 1826. Paris,
Louvre.

without the modifications and gradations of intermediate tones.
This came harshly to the eyes of those used to a comforting
pictorial dusk. Manet raised a curtain. Other painters were likewise engaged in drawing back the curtains. There were two
separate threads in the development of nineteenth-century
French Realism. The figure subject and its treatment became the
most immediately controversial development. But landscape had
its separate revolutionary factors. The realism of Constable had
given it an impetus in the Salon of 1824. Corot (1796–1875) in a
long career in which Constable may well have provided an
initial inspiration, became the patron saint of Impressionism
(Fig. 49).

Corot for a time—in the 1820s and 1830s—worked from nature
with a directness like that of Constable whose *Hay Wain* he
probably saw at the Salon of 1824. Though in the course of his
long life his work had other phases: the landscape with a classical
or romantic theme suitable for the Salon; the 'souvenirs' of the
1860s with their frail and fluttering delicacy; it was his direct
approach to nature at Barbizon and elsewhere that impressed and
influenced others.

From Corot, the painter of exquisite marines, Eugène Boudin
(1824–98) adopted the practice of painting in the open air in the
belief that this guaranteed a vivacity of effect not otherwise
obtainable. He has a place of importance in the history of Impressionism in having persuaded the young Claude Monet (1840–
1926) to join him in painting *en plein air* at Le Havre in 1858.
Together with the wandering Dutch painter, Johan Barthold
Jongkind (1819–91) they had already established a direction for
Realism in landscape when at the age of 22 Monet went to Paris
for further study. In the atelier of Gleyre he made friends with
those who were to be his allies in the Impressionist movement,
Alfred Sisley (1839–99) and Pierre Auguste Renoir. Their fellow-
student Frédéric Bazille (1841–70) was with them only in the

50. COURBET. The Wave. 1869. Edinburgh, National Gallery of Scotland.

51. HOKUSAI. The Wave from the 'Thirty-Six Views of Fujiyama'. About 1825–31. London, Victoria & Albert Museum.

movement's early stages, meeting an untimely end in the Franco-Prussian war.

The persecution of Manet and that unique event, the *Salon des Refusés* in 1863 where Napoleon III thought it politic, in view of many complaints of the Salon's unfairness, to order all the year's rejects to be shown, gave an impetus to new and radical ideas. Manet, with the *Déjeuner sur l'Herbe* was the hero of the *Refusés*. The group of friends and hero-worshippers who formed round him at the café he frequented were already the nucleus of an active group. Manet might be called the catalyst of Impressionism in bringing its members together without ever associating himself with the movement and the Impressionist exhibitions held from

52. CAMILLE PISSARRO. The Boieldieu Bridge, Rouen, at Sunset. 1896. City of Birmingham Art Gallery.

1874 onwards. He clung to the belief that the Salon, whatever its injustices, was the only correct place for exhibition. Nor had he the dominant interest in landscape shown by Monet, Sisley and Camille Pissarro (1830–1903). Yet there are technical threads of relationship which also illustrate the emergence of an Impressionist from a Realist technique.

The earlier Realists of Spain and Holland whom Manet first followed had not hesitated to use the darkest of tones and most violent oppositions of light and shade. Black shadows still characterized Courbet's efforts to give an equivalent of the weight and solid substance of reality. The 'discovery' of the Japanese colour print in the 1860s made a considerable difference to the outlook of artists in France (Fig. 50). At first these products of the popular *ukiyo-e* school of Japan and the fans, screens and other products of Japanese workmanship exported to Europe after the country was opened to commercial intercourse with the West, were fashionable curiosities. The screen and the print in the background of Manet's portrait of Zola in 1867–8 show the novelist and critic's up-to-dateness in taste.

The perceptive eyes of Manet and his friend Edgar Degas (1834–1917) saw more than a vogue in the prints by Hokusai (Fig. 51), Hiroshige, Utamaro and others that were now encountered everywhere in Paris. To a Japanese they might be of little account compared with the painting of the Kano school but to the nineteenth-century European they were a revelation. The very limitation of the process of printing from woodblocks in colour was an asset as regards colour. A small number of blocks, each providing a single flat tint gave the repetition and combination of a few selected colours which was the essential principle of harmony

Colour harmony of this kind had been difficult to achieve in European painting, concerned primarily with depths of tone, except for such a rare instance as the art of Vermeer provides. It is possible that a Far Eastern influence at Delft in Vermeer's time in the form of Chinese porcelain offered an escape from dark browns similar to the one nineteenth-century painters found in the light, flat colour of the artists of the *ukiyo-e* school. The effect on Manet was to lighten his palette and increase his sensitivity to colour. Retaining his Halsian directness of method he used flat areas of clear colour to give the contrast of light and shade.

It was the method Claude Monet adopted from him, an example being the fresh and sunny *Plage de Trouville* of 1870, already tending towards the Impressionist technique in its mature phase. Monet and his friends, Pissarro and Sisley, arrived at a system of colour harmony comparable with that of the Japanese though based on a different premise. It was their aim as landscape painters primarily to paint the reality of natural light and atmosphere enveloping a given space and not in a conventional disposition of light and dark (Fig. 52). It was logical to use those colours of which light was composed and to exclude the earth colours which had no part in the spectrum, excluding also white as the final sublimation of colour and black, the negation of light. Impression-

53. DEGAS. The Dance Rehearsal. 1873/4.
Glasgow Art Gallery, Burrell Collection.

ist painting thus became the art of translating light into the few
primary colours and their intermediaries. Although the practice of
working swiftly in the open to catch a particular atmospheric
moment did not allow of a consciously planned scheme, the
repetition and combination of the few colours made for harmony in
the same way as those of the Japanese print maker. The translation
of light and shade in terms of colour was empirically arrived at by
the great Impressionists but there was the instinctive 'rightness' of
the true artist in the result.

The Japanese print had an equal influence on European design
and composition. Its asymmetrical arrangement of forms permitted
a new freedom in the treatment of space within the picture area.
It enabled the Impressionist painters to preserve the value of a
coherent design even though their main purpose was to present an
effect of light in an entirely objective fashion. This coherence is a
concealed element in the work of Claude Monet. A first impression
may be of nature's own informality but plan becomes apparent in
the variety of interest his landscape compositions possess.

Three-dimensional realism also disguises the Eastern influence
in the figure paintings of Manet and his friend Edgar Degas, but
here again asymmetry contributes a structure to the casual and
unposed effects they sought both in portraits and in paintings of
everyday life. Degas in particular was inspired by the Japanese

54. RENOIR. Le Déjeuner des Canotiers. 1881.
Washington, The Phillips Collection.

print to the brilliance of spacing that gives movement to his
pictures of the ballet (Fig. 53).

The Japanese influence was persistent throughout the second
half of the century. It touched the watercolours and the one pure
landscape *Le Printemps* (Louvre), produced by Jean François
Millet (1814–75) in his later years, with an unwonted freshness.
Though James McNeill Whistler (1834–1903) disavowed realism
he took from Hiroshige the economy of colour and dominance of
blue that enabled him to convey so well the actuality of twilight on
the Thames; though basically his intention was abstract and
neither by painting direct from nature nor by the division of colour
did he conform to the Impressionist canon.

This was the canon steadfastly maintained by Monet and it says
much for his strength of purpose and character that for a time he
could draw two such independent characters as Manet and Renoir
(Fig. 54) into close accord with his outlook and method. After the
interruption of the Franco-Prussian war Monet worked at
Argenteuil then a pleasant village on the Seine. Renoir joined him
and Manet visited him also. It was perhaps the persuasion of
Berthe Morisot (1841–95), the greatly distinguished woman
Impressionist, that induced Manet to try his hand at *plein-air*
painting. At all events in what might be called the *annus mirabilis*

55. MONET. Gare St.-Lazare. 1877. Paris, Jeu de Paume Gallery.

56. J. M. W. TURNER. Rain, Steam and Speed. 1844. London, National Gallery.

of Impressionism, 1874, all three worked out of doors side by side.

Sunlight sparkled in their splendid canvases and yet the difference between them appears in the interest Manet and Renoir displayed in painting the Parisian holidaymakers at this scene of regattas, a cluster of sailing boats and waterside restaurants; whereas Monet was content with the shimmer of air and water. They give an example of the way in which great artists increasingly diverge as time goes on. Monet (Fig. 55) came at last to an abstraction of light and colour comparable with that of Turner (Fig. 56) in his final period; Manet to the superb rendering of the urban scene in the combination of humanity and still life of the *Bar aux Folies-Bergère* and Renoir to a neo-golden age of sun-flushed nudity projected in the paintings of his later years in the south of France.

8. *Modern Art in the Making*

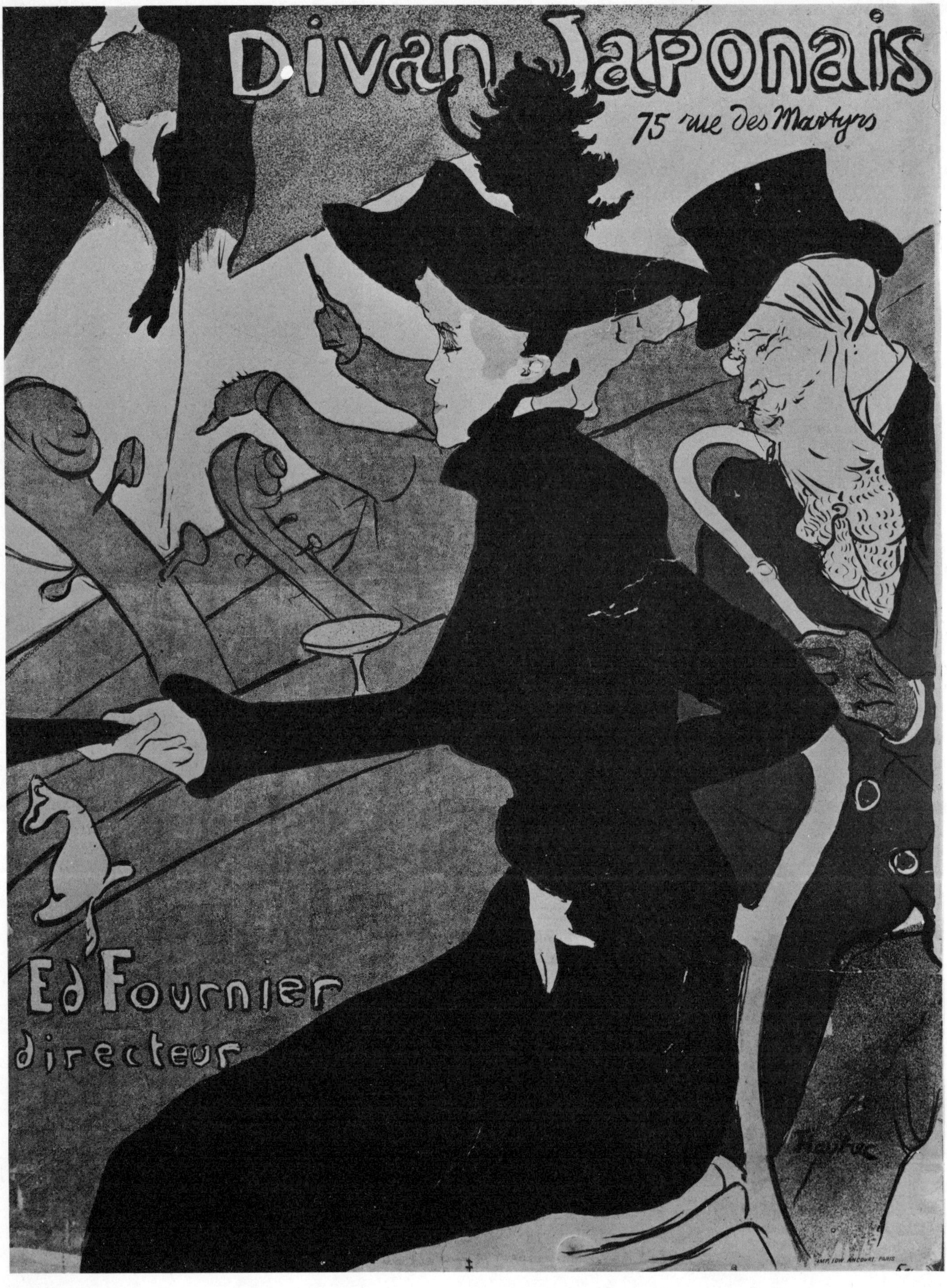
Divan Japonais
75 rue des Martyrs
Ed Fournier
directeur

The great and immediate forerunners of art in the twentieth century were Paul Cézanne (1839–1906), Paul Gauguin (1848–1903), Vincent van Gogh (1853–90) and Georges Seurat (1859–91). The first three are generally known as Post-Impressionists though in some ways this is a misleading description. The literal sense of 'coming after' the Impressionists does not apply to them seeing that such pillars of Impressionism as Degas, Monet and Renoir long outlived them. The term also makes too sharp a division of ideas and methods.

Modern art was a gradual development rather than a sudden change. Impressionism launched the evolution that branched out in various ways. It was an indispensable factor in the career of Cézanne. Through the advice and helpful teaching of Camille Pissarro he was set upon his mature course in the 1870s. The wild romanticism of his early days with its visions of rape, orgy and murder, its furious impasto and excesses both of violent colour and black shadow gave way to the self-discipline, the patient research and the meticulous use of thinly applied colour in his later paintings.

Cézanne's youthful violence is of interest in forecasting something of the freedom of *Fauve* colour as represented in the paintings of Henri Matisse (1869–1954) and his associates at the Fauvist Salon of 1905, André Derain (1880–1954) and Maurice Vlaminck (1876–1958). But this was not his vital contribution to modern painting, which (as he defined his ambition) was to make something durable out of Impressionism. He used, that is to say, the technique he learned from Pissarro to the end of representing structure rather than atmospheric effect. The motionless object, the 'still life' was his study instead of those transient aspects of light that Monet sought to catch in canvas after canvas devoted to the same subject at different times of day. Impressionism had schooled Cézanne to work from nature but nature as he saw it meant the solid form, whether of a mountain or of an apple. The Impressionist technique was of service in rendering the subtle differences of colour of the planes composing the surface of a three-dimensional shape. These were indications of the underlying architecture of natural forms it was Cézanne's aim to disclose.

A similarity has been found between these 'Post-Impressionist' artists in their lonely pursuit of art, isolated from the society of their time in the production of paintings that were either unknown, uncomprehended or detested. They were alike also in not resting content with the atmospheric realism of Monet, Sisley and Pissarro. This did not necessarily imply any want of admiration for those masters. Cézanne took pride in describing himself as a 'pupil of Pissarro'. Gauguin had an equal respect for one who had been his mentor also. In the days of his stock-market affluence, while still an amateur in painting, Gauguin had been an assiduous collector of paintings by the Impressionist group. The Post-Impressionists continued the Impressionist exploration of colour in their own fashion though there was a marked divergence in their aims and the values they arrived at.

VIII. TOULOUSE-LAUTREC. Le Divan Japonais. Poster. 1893.

Cézanne was the most classical in outlook; that is, in the conviction that the solid modelling of form was the essence of the painter's task (Fig. 57). It was the absence of such modelling in Gauguin's figure paintings that caused Cézanne to criticize them as mere silhouettes (*ombres Chinoises*). This was a purely technical comment on the method Gauguin evolved of painting with flat bright colour in boldly outlined areas. Gauguin's aim was more complex than this would suggest. He no longer assumed that the purpose of colour was realistically to give a record of what was seen in nature. It could alternatively be made symbolic of a state of mind or the character of an event (Fig. 58). A red ground was suggestive of conflict in his *Jacob wrestling with the Angel*. Livid hues were indicative of suffering and martyrdom in *Le Christ Jaune*.

Again, colour used at its maximum intensity could convey the full strength of the artist's own sensations instead of timidly reflecting what he saw. Georges Seurat had still another point of view. His approach to colour was scientific, a logical employment of the colours of the spectrum. Small dots of red, green, blue,

57. CÉZANNE. Self-portrait. About 1880.
Reinhart Collection, Winterthur.

orange, violet and yellow, variously grouped, could apparently combine in optical effect to give every desired nuance. This might seem the ultimate refinement of the analysis of light and shade carried out by Monet and his intimates and as such was a method Pissarro was persuaded for a while to employ. Monet on the other hand perceived that the resemblance to his own aims of this so-called 'Neo-Impressionism' was unreal. It might give a similar vibration of colour; on the other hand it was a laborious and quasi-mechanical process which inevitably disallowed the flexible variation and freedom of brush-stroke that imparted vivacity to Monet's own work. It was obvious, too, for the same reason, that it was an impossible method for that swift painting direct from nature that had been a main Impressionist activity.

Yet Seurat was a great though short-lived artist and his greatness was not based only on the method known as Pointillism or, as he preferred to call his stipple of colour, Divisionism. Like Cézanne he was much occupied with the thought of geometry but whereas Cézanne was concerned with its solid aspect as exemplified by the sphere, cone and cylinder, Seurat made use of verticals, horizontals and measured mathematical proportions of the plane surface to

58. GAUGUIN. Van Gogh at work. 1888. Amsterdam, Municipal Museum.

give unity of composition.

The geometrical design adds a calm grandeur to his landscapes of harbours, quays and river but he adapted it to different purposes according to his subject. There is the stiffness of the deportment of a bourgeois Sunday afternoon parade in his masterpiece, the *Grande Jatte*. Jagged forms give an appropriate sensation of acrobatic movement to *Le Cirque* and the repetition of forms carried to the verge of caricature invests his painting of a popular dance craze, *Le Chahut* (Fig. 59), with a touch of humour.

The artists so far mentioned had all contributed to one or other of the Impressionist exhibitions held during the period from 1874 to 1886—Cézanne to the first, Seurat to the last. Latecomers to the changing scene towards the end of the nineteenth century were Henri de Toulouse-Lautrec (1864–1901) and Vincent van Gogh. Lautrec's paintings of Parisian pleasure haunts were based in style on the work of Degas, though perhaps his greatest triumph was to bring into the colour lithograph a brilliance of design emanating from and rivalling that of the Japanese colour print.

Impressionist paintings, Japanese prints and the division of spectrum colour practised by Seurat all contributed to the decisive

59. Seurat. Le Chahut. 1889–90. Otterlo, Rijksmuseum Kröller-Müller.

change of style in Van Gogh's work after he arrived in Paris, a change from dark tones to glowing colour. It was his role to demonstrate in his short and sad life how much of personal emotion from sheer rapture to a desolating sense of tragedy it was within the capacity of painting to express (Fig. 60).

The force inherent in the great lonely figures who toiled in what would have seemed to most of their contemporaries a fruitless fashion was first an exciting discovery to a few of the younger generation. The painter Emile Bernard (1868–1941) was one of those in whom a fever of inquiry was aroused. He perceived the gathering power of Van Gogh during the latter's short stay in Paris from 1886 to 1888; he made a point of seeking out Cézanne at Aix; and was one of the group that formed round Gauguin on his visits to Pont-Aven. Perceptive also were the leaders of the forward-looking group of the 1890s called the Nabis, Paul Sérusier (1865–1927), who secured a demonstration from Gauguin of his ideas on colour, and the theorist and critic Maurice Denis (1870–1943).

A number of painters working on Pointillist lines, Seurat's friend, Paul Signac (1863–1935), Henri-Edmond Cross (1856–1910), Maximilien Luce (1858–1941) and others, helped to

60. Van Gogh. Garden of the Hospital at Arles. 1888–9. Reinhart Collection, Winterthur.

disseminate Seurat's idea of colour division though its possibilities in heightening the pictorical key were more fully and boldly exemplified by Van Gogh. He and Gauguin between them precipitated the first striking manifestation of the opening decade of the new century in the work of the *Fauves*—the 'wild beasts'— as a critic termed a group of younger artists whose works were hung together in the autumn Salon of 1905. Henri Matisse, André Derain and Maurice de Vlaminck were prominent in this group that gave colour an exuberant freedom. The break with Realism that had long been coming was made final in this dazzling explosion. The pace of change was now vastly accelerated. Active alliances of painters replaced the isolation of those who had struggled in obscurity. If their members were the subject of much criticism they were not overlooked. By the time the First World War began practically the whole course of modern art, as far as it can be traced in significant movements, had been mapped out.

Paris in the second half of the nineteenth century had become the unquestioned centre of European art and art training. In the first decade of the twentieth century young artists arrived from all parts of Europe to share in the stimulus of the ideas that were generated there. Some remained as members of the international 'School of Paris'. Others returned to their own country taking with them a pioneer message. The impact of Fauve colour was promptly felt in Russia (where Moscow merchants were among Matisse's first patrons) and in Germany. Still more influential was the Cubist movement which followed and supplanted Fauvism in notoriety and influence.

Cubism had two points of origin and two progenitors, the French artist Georges Braque (1882–1963) and the Spanish artist Pablo Picasso (b. 1881). The paintings of Cézanne, especially the late landscapes of Mont Sainte-Victoire in which the geometric planes were so trenchantly defined, together with his remarks on geometry as the artist's master key, gave one of the starting points. Cézanne's works, assembled in the Autumn Salon of 1904, and the year after his death in the memorial exhibition of 1907, made a deep impression. But the 'discovery' of African sculpture, almost as influential on painting in Paris as the Japanese print a half-century before, provided a reinforcement of ideas.

What was known as primitive art had long been the province of the anthropologist and regarded as without claim to aesthetic merit. Gauguin had been one of the first to appreciate the force it might possess, which he found in the rough peasant carvings of Brittany and in the native products of the South Seas. A growing interest in basic forms and first principles extended in the first years of the twentieth century to African folk sculpture. The planes so decisively carved, the powerful sense of structure in mask and fetish figure were a revelation to artists in France. The sphere, cone and cylinder of Cézanne had an alternative demonstration in works that came from Nigeria and the Congo.

With these guides to experimentation, and working in close accord, Braque and Picasso produced between 1907 and 1912 a

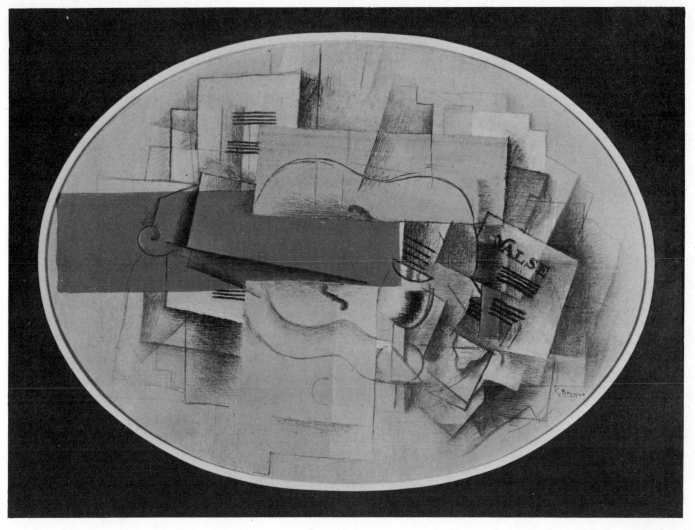

61. BRAQUE. Glass, Violin and Notes. 1913.
Cologne, Wallraf-Richartz-Museum.

62. PICASSO. The Three Musicians. 1921.
Philadelphia Museum of Art, A. E. Gallatin
Collection.

series of paintings in which subject steadily dwindled in importance
and the system of geometric planes grew dramatically more
dominant, penetrating the outer envelope of appearance with its
scaffolding until what remained were abstract forms overlapping
and intersecting. Yet this was only the beginning. The first
'analytic' stage of Cubism was followed by the 'synthetic' which
readmitted recognizable objects but used them with arbitrary
freedom (Fig. 62).

The Cubist still life, with its café table-tops, cards, newspapers
and mandolins, rearranged in a flat design, was typical of this
second phase (Fig. 61). The joint invention of Braque and Picasso
was *collage*, the addition to the painted designs of some piece of
reality, textile, wallpaper or newspaper heading—a practice that
has had a long subsequent history. Cubism, thus launched,
ceased to be simply the product of two individuals and became a
main instrument of new visual experience, employed by so many
artists that to detail its further progress would be to cover a large
area of modern art. It links together the mathematically precise
still life of Juan Gris (1887–1927) and the image of a machine age
defined by Fernand Léger (Fig. 63) (1881–1955). Its language of
style was adopted by the Italian Futurists to express their devotion
to the dynamic movement of the modern age and their rejection

63. FERNAND LÉGER. The Pink Tug. 1918.
Cologne, Wallraf-Richartz-Museum.

of past culture. The same language was so adaptable to twentieth-
century moods that it served the promoters of the Dada movement
in 1916 as a means of expressing their reaction against the purposes of the age and the violence in which the Futurists professed
to delight.

The geometry of Cubism was reduced to the austere rectangles
of Piet Mondrian (1872–1944) and other members of the De Stijl
group in Holland who regarded it as a common denominator for
design in many forms besides painting. In contrast, the rejection of
the normal reality of appearance opened the way to fantasy in
which Picasso in his Protean changes of style and temper has
offered a number of examples. Fantasy was the essence of the
Surrealist movement, the poet leader of which, André Breton,
revered Picasso as an associate genius, though Picasso was never
exclusively attached to any group and remained 'the magician of
surprise'.

At the opposite pole from the work of Picasso, that of Oskar
Kokoschka (b. 1886) is linked with the 'Expressionism' of Northern
Europe. In Europe generally stress on self-expression had for a
long time accompanied the wane of any public demand for
particular types of subject in painting. The pioneer of abstract art
Wassily Kandinsky (1866–1944) held that the beauty of art came

from 'an internal necessity'. He found an illustration even in so objective an art as that of the Impressionists, pointing out how little the subject mattered in one of Monet's paintings of haystacks, how important on the other hand was the way he applied colour. There was a beginning of appreciation also for the unrealistic reality that might exist in the mind of a simple and untutored artist of modern times as well as in a primitive society. In such an artist as Henri Rousseau (1844–1910), greatly admired by Picasso and his friends, there was a well of pure expression that a sophisticated training could only have spoilt (Fig. 64).

Expressionism implied some violence of colour or distortion of form in which personal emotions were revealed. These emotions were not necessarily gloomy though the sombre spirit of the Norwegian painter Edvard Munch (1863–1944) and the tragic intensity of Van Gogh's last paintings were especially influential in Germany. Violent colour distinguished the work of members of Die Brücke, a group founded at Dresden in 1905, Ernst Ludwig Kirchner (1880–1917), Karl Schmidt-Rottluff (b. 1884) and Emil Nolde (1867–1965). A second group of Expressionists that came together in Munich in 1911, the Blaue Reiter, was more

64. Henri ('Le Douanier') Rousseau. The Customs House. About 1900. London, Courtauld Institute Galleries.

abstract in tendency, Kandinsky playing a prominent part though Paul Klee (1879–1940), also one of the group, showed how the observation of nature might filter through the conscious (or sub-conscious) mind to emerge in some fascinating transformation.

Kokoschka who, after training in Vienna, experienced the atmosphere of Expressionism in Germany remained independent. He insisted on the value of expression (without the 'ism') as a healthy reaction to the external world, not only in indignant comment on human suffering and cruelty such as he made after the First World War but also in later delight in the pageant of nature and the panorama of cities. In an age baffled by its own progress when art gives signs of subordination to science and technology and does not escape sterility in abstraction, such reassertion of a vital interaction of nature and art has a special value.

List of illustrations

1. THE SPIRIT OF THE RENAISSANCE IN ITALY

I. FLORENCE. Piazza della Signoria: Loggia dei Lanzi.

1. MASACCIO: Adam and Eve Driven out of Paradise. About 1427. Florence, Santa Maria del Carmine.
   One of a series of frescoes that constitutes a key monument in early Renaissance art.

2. FRA FILIPPO LIPPI: Madonna and Child. Panel. About 1460. Florence, Uffizi.

3. SANDRO BOTTICELLI: Head of Venus. Detail from 'The Birth of Venus'. About 1486. Florence, Uffizi.
   The delicacy of technique in this painting is partly due to the fact that it is on linen rather than on panel.

4. MICHELANGELO: The Damned. Detail from 'The Last Judgement'. Fresco. 1536–41. Rome, Vatican, Sistine Chapel.

5. LUCA SIGNORELLI: Detail from 'The Last Judgement'. 1499–1502. Orvieto Cathedral.
   Signorelli's frescoes in Orvieto Cathedral are his most important single achievement.

6. RAPHAEL: Apollo and the Muses. Detail from 'The Parnassus'. 1508–11. Rome, Vatican, Stanza della Segnatura.
   One of the four frescoes in the Stanza della Segnatura which are widely regarded as one of the greatest achievements of High Renaissance art.

7. GIORGIONE: 'The Tempest'. Canvas. 1506–8. Venice, Accademia.
   The real meaning of this picture has always eluded scholars. Its present title was not given to the painting by the artist.

8. TITIAN: Venus of Urbino. Canvas. 1538. Florence, Uffizi.

9. LEONARDO DA VINCI: Detail. Madonna and Child with St. Anne. Cartoon. About 1507. London, National Gallery.
   This important work was purchased for the National Gallery in 1962 for £800,000.

10. ANTONIO CORREGGIO: The Sleep of Antiope. Canvas. 1521–2. Paris, Louvre.
    One of several mythological pictures by Correggio which exploit the voluptuous qualities of the female nude.

11. PIERO DELLA FRANCESCA: Detail of Angels from 'The Nativity'. Panel. 1474–8. London, National Gallery.
    One of the best preserved parts of a picture which in other areas is either unfinished or badly damaged.

12. ANDREA DEL CASTAGNO: The Last Supper. Fresco. 1445–50. Florence, Convent of Sant' Apollonia.
    Comparison with Leonardo's painting on the same subject shows the greater complexity and sophistication of Leonardo's design.

13. LEONARDO DA VINCI: The Last Supper. Fresco. 1495–7. Milan, Santa Maria delle Grazie.
    Leonardo's fresco was already in bad condition a few years after his death.

2. THE FLEMISH GENIUS

II. JAN VAN EYCK. Arnolfini Wedding Portrait. 1434. National Gallery, London.

14. QUENTIN METSYS: The Banker and His Wife. Panel. 1514. Paris, Louvre.

15. JEROME (HIERONYMUS) BOSCH: Detail from 'Hell', wing of triptych known as 'The Garden of Terrestrial Delights'. Panel. About 1500. Madrid, Prado.

16. PIETER BRUEGEL: Detail from 'The Triumph of Death'. Panel. About 1562. Madrid, Prado.
    Although paintings of this type by both Bruegel and Bosch are now admired for their great sense of fantasy and invention, they were originally meant to be judged within the framework of orthodox Roman Catholicism, and were partially intended as allegories on earthly vanities.

17. JACOB JORDAENS: Fecundity. Canvas. About 1625. Brussels, Musee des Beaux-Arts.

18. JAN BRUEGEL and RUBENS: Adam and Eve in Paradise. Panel. About 1620. The Hague, Mauritshuis.

19. PETER PAUL RUBENS: Detail from 'War and Peace'. Canvas. 1629–30. London, National Gallery.
    Paintings of this type were popular with sophisticated courtiers, for their classical education made mythological subjects easier to understand than is the case today.

3. THE DUTCH GENIUS

III. GERRIT BERKEHYDE. View of Haarlem with the Groote Kerk. 1674. Cambridge, Fitzwilliam Museum.

20. FRANS HALS: 'Malle Babbe' (Hille Bobbe). Canvas. About 1630–33. Berlin-Dahlem, Staatliche Museen.
    An interest in the fleeting qualities of facial expression is characteristic of seventeenth-century art.

21. REMBRANDT: The Night Watch. Canvas. 1642. Amsterdam, Rijksmuseum.
    The title 'The Night Watch' is strictly speaking inaccurate: the scene presented is taking place in the full light of day and shows Captain Frans Banning Cocq and his Company.

22. GERRIT LUNDENS: Copy about 1660 of Rembrandt's 'The Night Watch' in its original dimensions. Canvas. Amsterdam, Rijksmuseum. On loan from the National Gallery, London.

23. VAN DER HELST: The Banquet of the Civic Guard in Celebration of the Peace of Munster. Canvas. 1648. Amsterdam, Rijksmuseum.

24. GERARD VAN HONTHORST: Christ before the High Priest. Canvas. About 1620. London, National Gallery.

25. PIETER LASTMAN: Flight into Egypt. Panel. 1608. Rotterdam, Boymans-van Beuningen Museum.
    Most of Lastman's pictures are small in scale and brightly coloured.

26. NICOLAS MAES: Dreaming. Canvas. About 1655. Amsterdam, Rijksmuseum.

27. CAREL FABRITIUS: Self-portrait. Canvas. About 1650. Rotterdam, Boymans-van Beuningen Museum.
    Fabritius's early death in the explosion at Delft on 12 October, 1654, was a great loss for Dutch painting.

28. JAN VERMEER: The Letter. Canvas. About 1665. Amsterdam, Rijksmuseum.

4. THE SPANISH GENIUS

IV. VELAZQUEZ. Portrait of Juan de Pareja. 1650. New York, Metropolitan Museum of Art.

29. EL GRECO: Detail from 'The Burial of Count Orgaz'. Canvas. 1586. Toledo, Church of S. Tomé.
    This picture is still in the chapel for which it was painted.

30. JUSEPE DE RIBERA: Archimedes. Canvas. 1630. Madrid, Prado.

31. ESTEBAN MURILLO: Beggar Boy. Canvas. About 1645–55. Paris, Louvre.

32. FRANCISCO ZURBARÁN: St. Francis in Meditation. Canvas. About 1635–8. London, National Gallery.

33. DIEGO VELAZQUEZ: Aesop. Canvas. About 1638–41. Madrid, Prado.

5. THE DEVELOPMENT OF PORTRAITURE

V. TITIAN. Pope Paul III and his grandsons. 1546. Naples, Museo di Capodimonte.

34. HANS MEMLINC: Detail of donor from the 'Donne' Triptych. Panel. About 1477. London, National Gallery.
    It was often the custom in religious paintings before the eighteenth century to introduce into the scene depicted the person who had paid for the picture.

35. HANS HOLBEIN THE YOUNGER: Detail. Christina of Denmark, Duchess of Milan. Panel. 1538. London, National Gallery.
    This famous painting has recently been cleaned, and now the rich black satin dress stands out strongly against the brilliant blue background.

36. ANTHONY VAN DYCK: Queen Henrietta Maria, wife of Charles I. Canvas. 1638–9. Windsor Castle, Royal Collection. By gracious permission of Her Majesty the Queen.
    Contemporary eye-witness accounts of Henrietta Maria, who had extremely bad teeth, prove that Van Dyck's portraits of her, like those of her husband Charles I, were idealized.

37. SAMUEL COOPER: Barbara Villiers, Duchess of Cleveland. Miniature. 1661. Windsor Castle, Royal Collection. By gracious permission of Her Majesty the Queen.
    An unfinished portrait by the greatest of Restoration miniaturists.

38. FRANCIS HAYMAN: Hambleton Custance and Thomas Nuthall (?). Canvas. About 1750. Banbury, Upton House, National Trust (Bearsted Collection).

39. THOMAS GAINSBOROUGH: John Plampin of Chadacre. Canvas. About 1750–55. London, National Gallery.

40. JOSHUA REYNOLDS: Self-portrait. Canvas. About 1773. London, Royal Academy.
    This portrait cleverly reveals two of Reynolds' great enthusiasms: it is painted in a Rembrandtesque style and in the background is a bust of Michelangelo, whom Reynolds revered above all other artists.

6. THE DEVELOPMENT OF LANDSCAPE

VI. TURNER. Falls at Tivoli. c. 1818. London, Victoria and Albert Museum.

41. THOMAS GAINSBOROUGH: View of Dedham. Canvas. About 1750. London, Tate Gallery.

42. RICHARD WILSON: Ruins of the 'Villa of Maecenas', Tivoli. Canvas. About 1755. London, Tate Gallery.

43. THOMAS GIRTIN: Kirkstall Abbey, Yorkshire. Watercolour. 1800. London, Victoria & Albert Museum.

44. JOHN ROBERT COZENS: Alpine Scenery. Watercolour. 1776. London, Victoria & Albert Museum.

45. JOSEPH MALLORD WILLIAM TURNER: Source of the Arveyron. Watercolour. 1802–3. Mr. & Mrs. Paul Mellon Collection.

46. JOHN CROME: Mousehold Heath, Norwich. Canvas. About 1818. London, Victoria & Albert Museum.

47. JOHN CONSTABLE: Barge on the Stour. Oil on paper. About 1811. London, Victoria & Albert Museum.

7. REALISM TO IMPRESSIONISM

VII. COURBET. L'Atelier (Detail). 1854–55. Paris, Louvre.

48. EDOUARD MANET: La Musique aux Tuileries. Canvas. 1862. London, National Gallery.

49. JEAN BAPTISTE CAMILLE COROT: Pont de Narni. 1826. Paris, Louvre. A free oil-sketch (which would not have been exhibited during the artist's lifetime) for an elaborate composition, now in Ottawa, shown in the Paris Salon in 1827.

50. GUSTAVE COURBET: The Wave. Canvas. 1869. Edinburgh, National Gallery of Scotland.

51. KATSUSHIKA HOKUSAI: The Wave from the 'Thirty-Six Views of Fujiyama'. Colour print. About 1825–31. London, Victoria & Albert Museum.

52. CAMILLE PISSARRO: The Boieldieu Bridge, Rouen, at Sunset. Canvas. 1896. City of Birmingham Art Gallery.

53. EDGAR DEGAS: The Dance Rehearsal. Canvas. 1873/4. Glasgow Art Gallery, Burrell Collection.

54. PIERRE AUGUSTE RENOIR: Le Déjeuner des Canotiers. Canvas. 1881. Washington, The Phillips Collection.

55. CLAUDE MONET: Gare St.-Lazare. Canvas. 1877. Paris, Jeu de Paume Gallery.

56. JOSEPH MALLORD WILLIAM TURNER: Rain, Steam and Speed. Canvas. 1844. London, National Gallery.

8. MODERN ART IN THE MAKING

VIII. TOULOUSE-LAUTREC. Le Divan Japonais. Poster. 1893.

57. PAUL CÉZANNE: Self-portrait. Canvas. About 1880. Reinhart Collection, Winterthur.
    Of all the Impressionists, Cézanne and Van Gogh were the painters most obsessed by their own features.

58. PAUL GAUGUIN: Van Gogh at Work. Canvas. 1888. Amsterdam, Municipal Museum.

59. GEORGES SEURAT: Le Chahut. Canvas. 1889–90. Otterlo, Rijksmuseum Kröller-Müller.

60. VINCENT VAN GOGH: Garden of the Hospital at Arles. Canvas. 1888–9. Reinhart Collection, Winterthur.

61. GEORGES BRAQUE: Glass, Violin and Notes. Canvas. 1913. Cologne, Wallraf-Richartz-Museum.

62. PABLO PICASSO: The Three Musicians. Canvas. 1921. Philadelphia Museum of Art, A. E. Gallatin Collection.
    A perfect example of how Picasso reconciles an abstract style with the requirements of representation.

63. FERNAND LÉGER: The Pink Tug. Canvas. 1918. Cologne, Wallraf-Richartz-Museum.

64. HENRI ('LE DOUANIER') ROUSSEAU: The Customs House. Canvas. About 1900. London, Courtauld Institute Galleries.